Best

MAGAZINE

Design

28

SPD

th

Publication
Design
Annual

Contents

Leo Lionni: 12 He

President's Message 6

Photog

178

DESI

36

16

COV

28

rb Lubalin Award Winner

The Judges 8

ABOUT THE SOCIETY 7

152 *illustration*

Index 230

raphy

GN

GNERS

President's Message

*i*n his recent book, the eminent graphic designer Paul Rand criticizes the state of corporate design in America. He mourns the passing of the design-conscious chiefs of CBS, Arco Oil, Westinghouse, Container Corporation of America, Olivetti, and IBM— world, "management does not really appreciate the contributions that design can make socially, esthetically, and economically."

I'm glad to say that in one critical area— ours— Mr. Rand's point does not apply. As you will see in these pages, today's magazines are filled with exciting and innovative illustration, typography, and photography. And editors and publishers (the corporate structure) at these magazines seem to be more aware than ever of the crucial centrality been better understood or more universally acknowledged.

With this recognition comes increased responsibility, intensified by a generally dismal economic climate as well as increasing competition from other visual media. The pressure is indeed on, but art directors all over the country are rising to the challenge and producing the kind of work that makes editors and publishers (our "corporate chiefs") recognize good design's contribution to their magazines—socially, esthetically, and economically.

We're not always aware, in our daily work lives, of this widespread appreciation of our efforts. But it really is there: SPD has received generous support in the past three years from major magazine publishing companies. Their contributions are a recognition of the importance of SPD's programs, and are most of all a tribute to the designers and art directors whose work sustains and illuminates the vitality of their magazines.

Walter Bernard
President

About The Society

established in 1965, the Society of Publication Designers was formed to acknowledge the role of the art director/designer in the creation and development of the printed page. The art director as journalist brings a visual representation to the editorial mission to clarify and enhance the written word. This graphic-design skill is developed and specialized, presenting endless challenges in the current technological advancements of the publishing industry.

The Society provides for its members a monthly Speaker's Luncheon; a Speaker's Evening series; a bimonthly newsletter, GRIDS; the publication design annual; the Design Exhibition held annually at the Jacob Javits Center in conjunction with the International GRAFIX EXPO; studio and magazine tours for art directors and designers, and an annual SPOTS Competition and Exhibition for illustrators. It also actively participates in related activities that bring together members of the numerous design communities in the New York area.

The Society of Publication Designers Annual Competition draws several thousand entries from the United States and abroad. A jury of top designers, chosen for their distinguished expertise in design, judge the submitted works in seventy-five categories.

Once the finest works have been selected to appear in the Exhibition and the publication design annual, the jury awards Gold and Silver medals, the highest awards for editorial design. The remaining winners receive the distinction of merit and create, by their diversity, a compendium of the best-designed pieces from the submitted entries in design, photography, and illustration.

The Publication Design Annual, published by Rockport Publishing, is a volume containing the award-winning designs from the yearly competition. It is an invaluable reference for designers, educators, students, corporate communicators, editors, publishers, and all others engaged in the various aspects of editorial design.

Photos: © Davies & Starr

RHONDA RUBINSTEIN
Art Director
ESQUIRE

B.W. HONEYCUTT
Art Director
DETAILS

Photos: © Davies & Starr

KAREN BLOOM (CHAIR)
Manager, Public Relations
WESTVACO CORPORATION

KENT HUNTER
Creative Director
FRANKFURT, GIPS, BALKIND

JANE PALACEK
Art Director
HEALTH

GAIL ANDERSON
Deputy Art Director
ROLLING STONE

GARY KOEPKE
Principal
KOEPKE DESIGN, INC.

DON MORRIS (CHAIR)
Principal
DON MORRIS DESIGN

JUDY GARLAN
Art Director
ATLANTIC MONTHLY

CHRIS GANGI
Art Director
CONDÉ NAST TRAVELER

MICHAEL GROSSMAN
Design Director
ENTERTAINMENT WEEKLY

JOEL BERG
Art Director
HARPER'S BAZAAR

Photos: © Davies & Starr

TOM BENTKOWSKI (CHAIR)
Design Director
LIFE

FO WILSON
Principal
STUDIO W

MICHAEL KEEGAN
Art Director
THE WASHINGTON POST

LISA THACKABERRY
Photo Editor
LOS ANGELES TIMES

DOUGLAS TURSHEN
Design Director
FAMILY CIRCLE

CAROLINE BOWYER (CHAIR)
Art Director
ELLE DECOR

HELENE SILVERMAN
Principal
HELLO STUDIO

BRUCE RAMSAY
Art Director
MIRABELLA

CHARLES DIXON
Art Director
BLACK ENTERPRISE

LUCY SISMAN
Art Director
ALLURE

Leo Lionni: Herb Lubalin Award Winner

N E W   P O S S I B I L I T I E S …in seven decades working as a graphic designer, art director, photographer, painter, sculptor, editor, filmmaker, teacher, and children's book author, Leo Lionni has maintained an unflagging interest in new possibilities, new challenges, new ways of expressing his immense talents. Born in Amsterdam to Dutch parents, Lionni was inspired from childhood by two artistic uncles (one an art collector, the other an architect/portraitist). Although he received his doctorate in economics from the University of Genoa, his interest in art took precedence over the world of business. Moving to Milan with his wife, Nora, he painted abstract canvases and was invited to exhibit with the Futurists by F. T. Marinetti. Although "there was no such term as art director," Lionni opened an office designing ads and posters for Motta, one of Italy's leading pastry makers, with such talents as A. M. Cassandre, Herbert Matter and Xanti Schwinsky.

Lionni's Jewish background was cause for his emigration from Fascist Italy to the U.S. in 1939. Impressed with Lionni's urbane wit and intelligence, Charles Coiner hired him as art director at N.W. Ayer of Philadelphia, where he was largely responsible for the use of fine artists Henry Moore and Fernand Leger in advertising for Container Corporation, among others. In 1947 he had his first one-man show of paintings in the U.S. at Norlyst Gallery in Manhattan.

Lionni moved to New York in 1949 and succeeded Will Burtin as art director at Fortune magazine, continuing to fulfill Henry Luce's promise that it be, "if possible the undisputed most beautiful…magazine as exists in the United States." Working to this end until 1961, Lionni redesigned Fortune in collaboration with Walter Allner, distinctly changing the editorial personality to embrace the work of photographers such as Walker Evans, Dan Weiner, Arnold Newman, and Martin Munkacsi, as well as illustrators including Ben Shahn, Robert Osborn, and Antonio Frasconi.

Photo: © Davies & Starr

During this prolific time, Lionni also designed ads for CBS, book jackets for Vintage and Doubleday, and the book of Edward Steichen's landmark Museum of Modern Art exhibition, The Family of Man. As design director for Olivetti of America, he contributed architectural, interior, and exhibition design along with ads and promotion pieces. He co-founded the International Design Conference in Aspen, organized the design department at Parsons School of Design, NYC, and in 1955, became co-editor of Print magazine. His first children's book, begun as an improvised story to entertain his children on a dull train ride, was published as Little Blue and Little Yellow in 1959.

Returning to Italy after leaving Fortune in 1961, Lionni became editor of Panorama for Time-Life. He continues to write, sculpt, and paint—as seen in many one-man shows in Italy, Germany, and the U.S.—as well as produce dozens of popular children's books.

The Society awarded the Herb Lubalin Award for continuing excellence in publication design to Leo Lionni, on May 7, 1993 at the twenty-eighth annual Awards Gala held at the New York Public Library. This honor is awarded by vote of the Board of Directors of SPD, to a designer whose work has had a significant impact in the design field, and most especially for "continuing excellence on the field of publication design."

Past recipients of this prestigious award have been Milton Glaser, Bradbury Thompson, Henry Wolf, Frank Zachary, B. Martin Pedersen, Cipe Pineles Burtin, Will Hopkins, Rochelle Udell, and Lou Silverstein.

In this issue:
THE POLITICS OF ALUMINUM

FORTUNE

January 1958

In this issue: *Radio Astronomy*
Curtiss-Wright
The White House Since Sputnik

Alan Fletcher

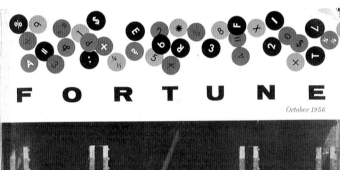

FORTUNE

October 1956

FORTUNE

January 1959

Beginning in this issue:
An Exploration of
"The Markets of the 1960's"

Fortune

July 1954

In this issue: Eastman Kodak Enlarged ∙ Businessmen in Washington
An Executive Retires —They Asked for It
Monorail for Your City? *And twenty other timely articles—see page 1*

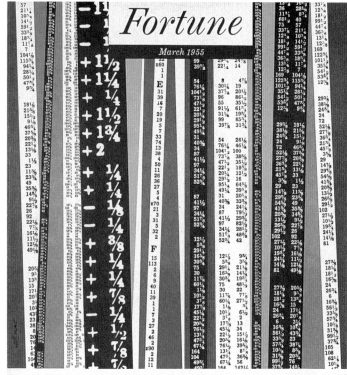

Fortune

March 1955

In this issue: The Future Market for Stocks Inside Campbell Soup
Mysteries of Delegation The Next Great Synthetic
How to Prolong a Depression *And twenty other timely articles—see page 1*

Beginning a new series: U.S. Business in the World Markets

Lionni

1910: Born in Amsterdam.

1925: Family moves to Italy.

1931: Marries Nora Maffi. Invited by Marinetti to join Futurists. Son Louis born.

1935: Ph.D. in Economics, University of Genoa.

1931-39: Painting, advertising, design, and writing, Milan.

1938: Son Paolo born.

1939: Emigrates to U.S.

1939-47: Art director with N.W. Ayer & Son, Philadelphia. Art director for Container Corporation, Chrysler Corporation, *Ladies' Home Journal*, General Electric Company. Posters for Office of Emergency Management. Design consultant for Federal Housing Administration.

1946: Instructor of design, Black Mountain College (NC) Summer Art Institute.

1947: First one-man show of paintings, Norlyst Gallery, NYC.

1947-48: Painting and study in Europe.

1949: Art director, Fortune. Design director, Olivetti Corporation of America. Consultant, American Cancer Society.

1951: Cofounder, Aspen Design Conference. Redesign of *Fortune* format.

1953: Chairman, International Design Conference, Aspen.

1954: Exhibition (*Four American Graphic Designers*), Museum of Modern Art. Organizes Design Department, Parsons School of Design.

1955: Co-editor, with Lawrence Audrain, *Print*. Art Director *Print*, President, AIGA. Named Art Director of the Year by National Society of Art Directors. Art director, *The Family of Man* book of the photographic exhibition at The Museum of Modern Art. Design of Olivetti showroom in San Francisco.

1956: *Resurgent India*, a Fortune photographic portfolio Design of Olivetti showroom in Chicago.

1957: One-man show, American Institute of Graphic Arts. Design of *Unfinished Business* American Pavilion at the Brussels World Fair.

1960: First children's book, *Little Blue and Little Yellow. Designs for the Printed Page* for Fortune.

1961: Moves to San Bernardo, Lavagna, Italy.

1962-1963: Editor, *Panorama*, for Time-Life.

1967: Five first-awards, Teheran International Film Festival, for animated cartoon *Swimmy*.

1972: First one-man exhibition of bronzes, drawings, paintings, prints related to botany theme, Milan, Verona, and Turin. Venice Biennial (International Sculpture Exhibition; International Drawings Exhibition). *Parallel Botany* published by Alfred A. Knopf.

1974: New York Art Directors Hall of Fame.

1976-1980: Italian, German, and Japanese editions of *Parallel Botany* published.

1981: Japan Foundation invitation-grant to Japan.

1983: Named to Cooper Union Faculty of Humanities and Social Sciences.

1984: Gold Medal from the American Institute of Graphic Arts.

1991: Honorary Doctor of Fine Arts degree, Cooper Union.

1993: Retrospective at the Herb Lubalin Center, Cooper Union.

1993: Herb Lubalin Award, Society of Publication Designers.

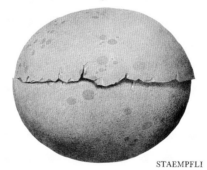

LEO LIONNI   *new drawings*

STAEMPFLI

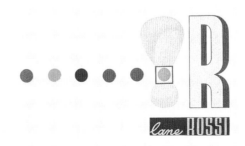

Cane ROSSI

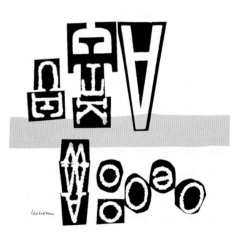

Print

IX:5

Covers

CONSUMER
TRADE

Annual Report

Corporate

NEWSPAPER

Detail from
photograph by
George Holz for
Men's Journal

Publication Esquire
Award Silver
Art Director Rhonda Rubinstein
Designer Rhonda Rubinstein
Illustrator Barbara Kruger
Photographer Dave Pokress
Photo Editor Betsy Horan
Publisher The Hearst Corporation
Category Cover
Date May 1992

Publication Time International
Award Silver
Design Director Arthur Hochstein
Art Director Rudolph C. Hoglund
Illustrator Wilson McLean
Publisher Time/Warner, Inc.
Category Cover
Date February 13, 1992

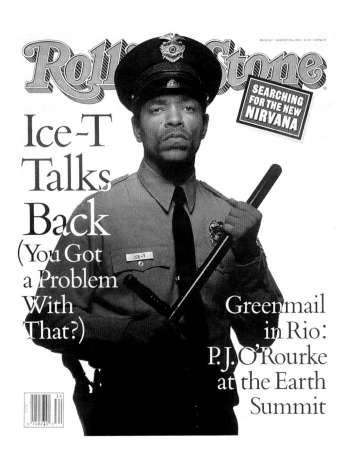

Publication Rolling Stone
Award Silver
Art Director Fred Woodward
Photographer Mark Seliger
Photo Editor Laurie Kratochvil
Publisher Straight Arrow Publishers, Inc.
Category Cover
Date August 20, 1992

Publication Esquire
Award Silver
Art Director Rhonda Rubinstein
Designer Rhonda Rubinstein
Publisher The Hearst Corporation
Category Cover
Date February 1992

Publication   Entertainment Weekly
Award   Silver
Design Director   Michael Grossman
Art Director   Mark Michaelson
Designer   Michael Grossman
Photographer   Mark Hanauer
Photo Editors   Mary Dunn, Doris Brautigan
Publisher   Entertainment Weekly, Inc.
Category   Cover
Date   June 19, 1992

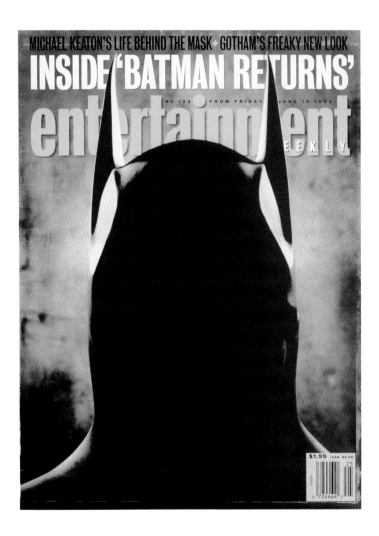

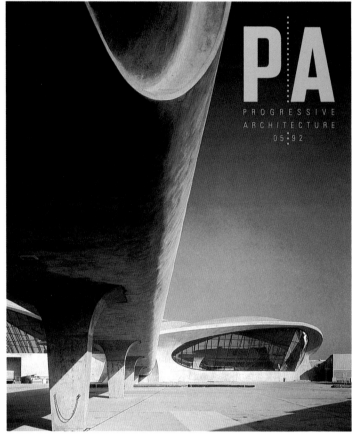

Publication   Progressive Architecture
Award   Silver
Art Director   Derek Bacchus
Designer   Kristin Reid
Photographer   Ezra Stoller/Esto
Publisher   Penton Publishing
Category   Cover
Date   May 1992

Publication	Los Angeles Times Magazine
Award	Silver
Art Director	Nancy Duckworth
Designer	Nancy Duckworth
Photographer	Mark Seliger
Photo Editor	Lisa Thackaberry
Publisher	Los Angeles Times
Category	Cover
Date	May 10, 1992

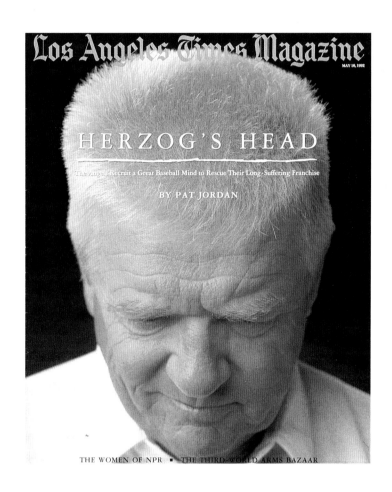

Los Angeles Times Magazine

MAY 10, 1992

HERZOG'S HEAD

The Angels Recruit a Great Baseball Mind to Rescue Their Long-Suffering Franchise

BY PAT JORDAN

THE WOMEN OF NPR ■ THE THIRD-WORLD ARMS BAZAAR

Publication a/r/c
          Architectural Research and Criticism
Award Merit
Art Director Arthur Niemi
Designer Arthur Niemi
Publisher Atlas of the City
Studio Atlanta Art and Design Inc.
Client Greg Crysler
Category Cover
Date Summer/Fall 1992

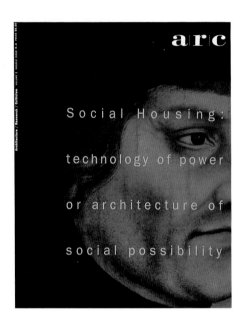

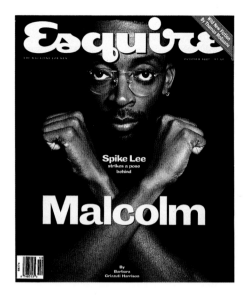

Publication Esquire
Award Merit
Design Director Rhonda Rubinstein
Art Director Rhonda Rubinstein
Photographer Frank Ockenfels 3
Photo Editor Betsy Horan
Publisher The Hearst Corporation
Category Cover
Date October 1992

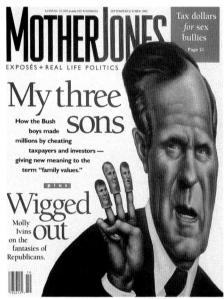

Publication Mother Jones
Award Merit
Art Director Kerry Tremain
Designer Kerry Tremain
Illustrator Anita Kunz
Publisher Foundation for National Progress
Category Cover
Date September/October 1992

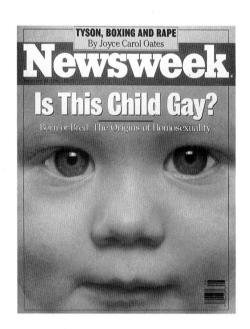

Publication Newsweek
Award Merit
Art Director Patricia Bradbury
Designer Peter Comitini
Photographer Penny Gentieu
Publisher Newsweek, Inc.
Category Cover
Date February 24, 1992

Publication Newsweek
Award Merit
Art Director Patricia Bradbury
Designer Peter Comitini
Publisher Newsweek, Inc.
Category Cover
Date May 18, 1992

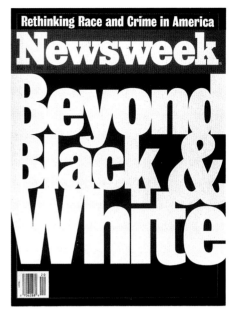

Publication Newsweek
Award Merit
Art Director Patricia Bradbury
Designers Mark Inglis, Ron Meyerson
Illustrator Lou Brooks
Publisher Newsweek, Inc.
Category Cover
Date December 7, 1992

Publication	New York
Award	Merit
Design Director	Robert Best
Designers	Robert Best, Syndi Becker
Photographer	Ted Hardin
Photo Editor	Jordan Schaps, Margery Goldburg
Publisher	K-III Magazines
Category	Cover
Date	June 1, 1992

Publication	New York
Award	Merit
Design Director	Robert Best
Art Director	Syndi Becker
Designer	Syndi Becker
Illustrator	Gary Halgren
Publisher	K-III Magazines
Category	Cover
Date	July 20, 1992

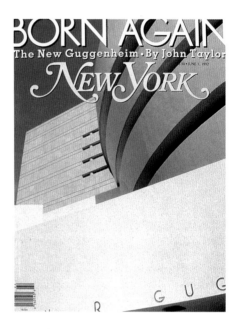

Publication	Snake Eyes
Award	Merit
Designer	Jonathon Rosen
Illustrator	Jonathon Rosen
Publisher	Fantagraphic Books
Studio	Jonathon Rosen
Category	Cover
Date	February 1992

Publication	How
Award	Merit
Art Director	Carole Winters
Designer	David Carson
Publisher	F&W Publications
Category	Cover
Date	April 1992

Publication Total TV
Award Merit
Art Director Jill Armus
Illustrator Josh Gosfield
Photo Editor Heather Alberts
Publisher Total TV, Inc.
Category Cover
Date December 1992

Publication Ray Gun
Award Merit
Design Director David Carson
Designer David Carson
Illustrator Larry Carroll
Photographer Steve Sherman
Studio David Carson Design
Publisher Ray Gun
Category Cover
Date November 1992

Publication Young Sisters and Brothers
Award Merit
Design Director Fo Wilson
Designer Fo Wilson
Publisher Paige Publications, Inc.
Studio Studio W
Category Cover
Date June/July 1992

Publication Ray Gun
Award Merit
Design Director David Carson
Designer David Carson
Illustrator Josh Gosfield
Publisher Ray Gun
Studio David Carson Design
Category Cover
Date November 1992

Publication Sports Illustrated
Award Merit
Design Director Steven Hoffman
Designer Craig Gartner
Photographer John Iacono
Photo Editor Heinz Kluetmeier
Publisher Time Inc. Magazine Company
Category Cover
Date May 18, 1992

Publication Sports Illustrated
Award Merit
Design Director Steven Hoffman
Designer F. Darrin Perry
Illustrator Peter Read Miller
Photographer Peter Read Miller
Photo Editor Heinz Kluetmeier
Publisher Time Inc. Magazine Company
Category Cover
Date January 6, 1992

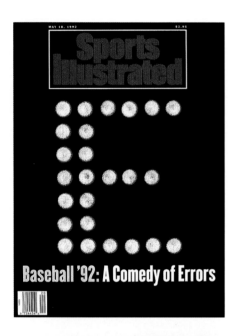

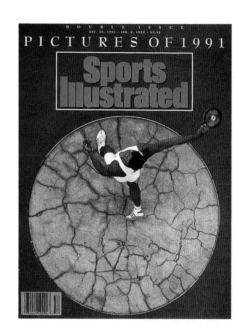

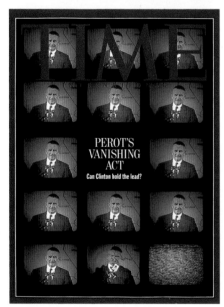

Publication Time International
Award Merit
Design Director Arthur Hochstein
Art Director Rudolph C. Hoglund
Photographer Alex Quesada Matrix
Publisher Time Inc.
Category Cover
Date July 27, 1992

Publication Sports Illustrated
Award Merit
Design Director Steven Hoffman
Designer F. Darrin Perry
Illustrator Peter Read Miller
Photographer Peter Read Miller
Photo Editor Heinz Kluetmeier
Publisher Time Inc. Magazine Company
Category Cover
Date November 16, 1992

Publication Time International
Award Merit
Design Director Arthur Hochstein
Art Director Rudolph C. Hoglund
Illustrator Joe Lertola
Photographer Hans Verhufen
Publisher Time Inc.
Category Cover
Date March 9, 1992

Publication W
Award Merit
Creative Director Dennis Freedman
Design Director Owen Hartley
Art Director Kirby Rodriguez
Photographer Matthew Rolston
Publisher Fairchild Publications
Category Cover
Date April 13, 1992

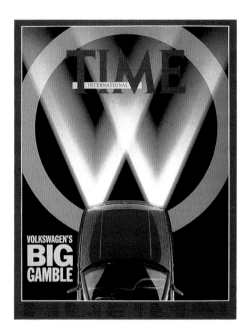

Publication Condé Nast Traveler
Award Merit
Design Director Diana La Guardia
Designer Christin Gangi
Photographer Brigitte Lacombe
Publisher Condé Nast Publishing Co., Inc.
Category Cover
Date January 1992

Publication Architectural Record
Award Merit
Design Director Alberto Bucchianeri
Designer Alberto Bucchianeri
Photographer Grant Mudford
Publisher McGraw-Hill Publications
Category Cover
Date February 1992

Publication Calligraphy Review
Award Merit
Design Director Erena Rae
Illustrator Seymour Chwast
Studio The Pushpin Group Inc.
Category Cover
Date Spring 1992

Publication Graphis
Award Merit
Design Director B. Martin Pedersen
Art Directors B. Martin Pedersen, Randall Pearson
Designer B. Martin Pedersen
Illustrator John Mattos
Publisher Graphis US, Inc.
Category Cover
Date September/October 1992

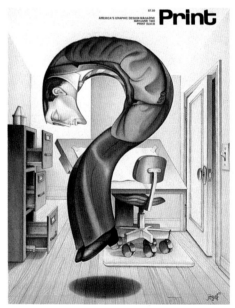

Publication Graphis
Award Merit
Design Director B. Martin Pedersen
Art Directors B. Martin Pedersen, Randell Pearson
Designer B. Martin Pedersen
Illustrator Mick Haggerty
Publisher Graphis US, Inc.
Category Cover
Date July/August 1992

Publication Print
Award Merit
Design Director Andrew Kner
Art Director Andrew Kner
Designer Jözef Sumichrast
Illustrator Jözef Sumichrast
Publisher RC Publications
Category Cover
Date May/June 1992

Publication Progressive Architecture
Award Merit
Art Director Derek Bacchus
Designer Julie Anne Yee
Photographer Marvin Rand
Publisher Penton Publishing
Category Cover
Date September 1992

Publication TDC
Award Merit
Design Director John Lyle Sanford
Designer John Lyle Sanford
Photographer Skip Brown
Publisher Discovery Publishing, Inc.
Category Photography/Photojournalism, Portraits
Date March 1992

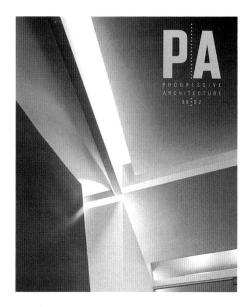

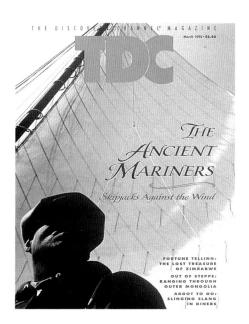

Publication Progressive Architecture
Award Merit
Art Director Derek Bacchus
Designer Julie Anne Yee
Publisher Penton Publishing
Category Cover
Date October 1992

Publication Saint Francis Hospital Spirit
Award Merit
Design Director Daphne Geismar
Art Director Daphne Geismar
Designer Daphne Geismar
Photographer Bill West
Studio Context Incorporated.
Category Cover
Date Spring 1991

Publication Anchorage Daily News
Award Merit
Design Director Galie Jean-Louis
Art Director Galie Jean-Louis
Designer Galie Jean-Louis
Illustrator Scott Menchin
Publisher Anchorage Daily News
Studio Scott Menchin
Category Cover
Date August 1992

Publication Eastsideweek
Award Merit
Art Director Sandra Schneider
Photographer Karen Moskowitz
Publisher Sasquatch Publishing
Category Cover
Date September 2, 1992

Publication Eastsideweek
Award Merit
Art Director Sandra Schneider
Illustrator Glynis Sweeny
Publisher Sasquatch Publishing
Category Cover
Date October 28, 1992

Publication Minnesota Guide
Award Merit
Art Director Lynn Phelps
Designer Lynn Phelps
Illustrator Tom R. Garrett
Photographer Mike Valeri
Publisher Star Tribune
Category Cover
Date April 1992

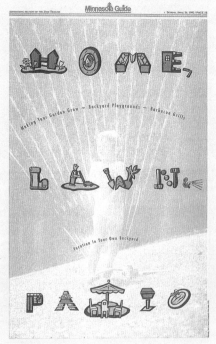

Publication The New York Times/Sophisticated Traveler
Award Merit
Art Director Nicki Kalish
Designer Nicki Kalish
Illustrator Josh Gosfield
Publisher The New York Times
Category Cover
Date October 18, 1992

Publication The Boston Globe/Special Section
Award Merit
Art Director Rena Sokolow
Designer Rena Sokolow
Photographer Toyohiro Yamada/ FPG
Publisher The Boston Globe Publishing Co.
Category Cover
Date March 29, 1992

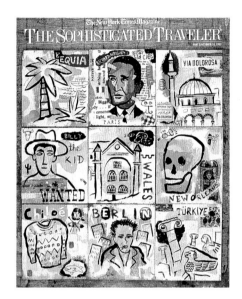

Publication The Boston Globe Magazine
Award Merit
Art Director Lucy Bartholomay
Designer Lucy Bartholomay
Illustrator Anthony Russo
Publisher The Boston Globe Publishing Co.
Category Cover
Date December 27, 1992

Publication Los Angeles Times Magazine
Award Merit
Art Director Nancy Duckworth
Photographer William Duke
Photo Editor Lisa Thackaberry
Publisher Los Angeles Times
Category Cover
Date June 14, 1992

Publication The New York Times Magazine
Award Merit
Art Director Janet Froelich
Designer Kandy Littrell
Photographer Sally Mann
Photo Editor Kathy Ryan
Publisher The New York Times
Category Cover
Date September 27, 1992

Publication The New York Times Magazine
Award Merit
Art Director Janet Froelich
Designer Kathi Rota
Illustrator Ralph Staedman
Photo Editor Kathy Ryan
Publisher The New York Times
Category Cover
Date November 1, 1992

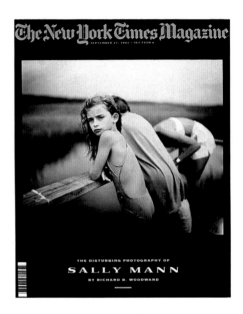

Publication The New York Times Magazine
Award Merit
Art Director Janet Froelich
Designer Kandy Littrell
Photographer Jon Jones
Photo Editor Kathy Ryan
Publisher The New York Times
Category Cover
Date July 26, 1992

Publication The New York Times Magazine
Award Merit
Art Director Janet Froelich
Designer Charlene Benson
Photographer Silvia Otte
Photo Editor Kathy Ryan
Publisher The New York Times
Category Cover
Date September 13, 1992

Publication The New York Times Magazine
Award Merit
Art Director Janet Froelich
Designer Kandy Littrell
Photographer Michael O'Neill
Photo Editor Kathy Ryan
Publisher The New York Times
Category Cover
Date November 15, 1992

Publication The New York Times Magazine
Award Merit
Art Director Janet Froelich
Photographer Michael O'Brien
Photo Editor Kathy Ryan
Publisher The New York Times
Category Cover
Date January 19, 1992

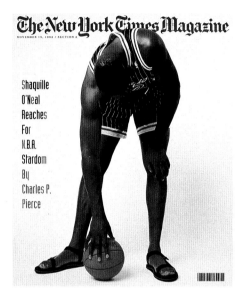

Publication Shiny
Award Merit
Design Director Dirk Rowntree
Art Director Dirk Rowntree
Illustrator Patti Martori
Photo Editor Dirk Rowntree
Publisher Shiny International
Category Cover
Date July/August

Publication The Washington Post Magazine
Award Merit
Art Director Richard Baker
Designer Richard Baker
Photographer Pete McArthur
Photo Editor Karen Tanaka
Publisher The Washington Post Co.
Category Cover
Date April 12, 1992

Publication The Washington Post Magazine
Award Merit
Art Director Richard Baker
Designer Kelly Doe
Illustrator Peter DeSeve
Publisher The Washington Post Co.
Category Cover
Date December 20, 1992

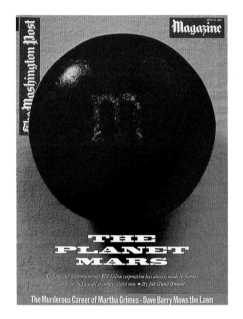

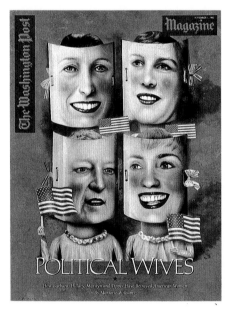

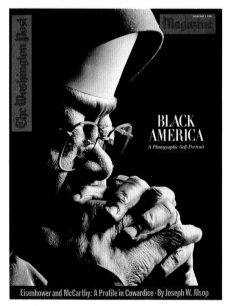

Publication The Washington Post Magazine
Award Merit
Art Director Richard Baker
Designer Kelly Doe
Illustrator Janet Woolley
Publisher The Washington Post Co.
Category Cover
Date November 1, 1992

Publication The Washington Post Magazine
Award Merit
Art Director Richard Baker
Designer Richard Baker
Photographer Dixie D. Vereen
Photo Editor Deborah Needleman
Publisher The Washington Post Co.
Category Cover
Date February 2, 1992

Publication The Phildelphia Inquirer
Award Merit
Art Director Jessica Helfand
Illustrator Scott Menchin
Publisher The Philadelphia Inquirer
Category Cover
Date August 1992

INSIDE: FIGHTING THOSE A #%(@! COMPUTER GALLS

INQUIRER

AUGUST 2, 1992

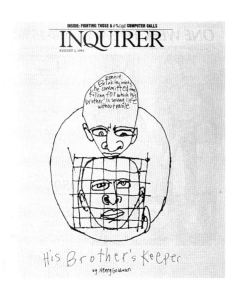

His Brother's Keeper
by Henry Goldman

The New York Times
Arts & Leisure

Sunday, November 15, 1992 Section 2

Malcolm X: The Facts, the Fictions, the Film

A Museum Grows in Brooklyn (Painfully)

Publication The New York Times/
Arts & Leisure
Award Merit
Design Director Tom Bodkin
Art Director Linda Brewer
Designer Linda Brewer
Illustrator Rico Lins
Publisher The New York Times
Category Newspapers/Front Page
Date November 15, 1992

May 26, 1992 • Vol. XXXVII No. 21 • The Weekly Newspaper of New York • $1.00
ENOUGH ALREADY: JOHNNY CARSON'S LONG GOODBYE (GARY INDIANA, P.51)
'LETHAL WEAPON 3': KICK SOME ASS & YOUR MIND WILL FOLLOW (LEVY, P.70)
PBS: MADE IMPOSSIBLE BY A GRANT FROM BIG BUSINESS (LEDBETTER, P.37)

the village VOICE

THE 1992 OBIE AWARDS
Theater (P.105)

The Perils of Perot

How Do You
Think He Made
$3 Billion, Anyway?

BY MICHAEL TOMASKY (P.27)

Publication The Village Voice
Award Merit
Design Director Robert Newman
Designer Florian Bachleda
Illustrator Philip Burke
Publisher Village Voice
Publishing Corporation
Category Newspapers/Front Page
Date May 26, 1992

December 28, 1992 • Vol. XXXVII No. 52 • The Weekly Newspaper of New York • $1.00
THE MAN WHO WOULD BE MAXWELL: LEDBETTER ON ZUCKERMAN (P.27)
THE LIMITS OF CONSENT: HOUPPERT ON THE GLEN RIDGE TRIAL (P.31)
IS A CROWN HEIGHTS HASIDIC CHARITY ABOVE THE LAW? (METRO, P.14)

the village VOICE

A GALLERY DEFINES THE MOMENT
(Hess on Exit Art, P.95)

Appears to Blind Girl at Night
JESUS SEEN IN NEW HAVEN

Artist's Rendering

Amazed Onlookers See the Madonna and Satan

BEARING WITNESS IN WOOSTER SQUARE
BY KATHY DOBIE, P.33

SYCAMORE TREE REVEALS HIS IMAGE

No Sign of Elvis

Publication The Village Voice
Award Merit
Design Director Robert Newman
Publisher Village Voice
Publishing Corporation
Category Newspapers/Front Page
Date December 12, 1992

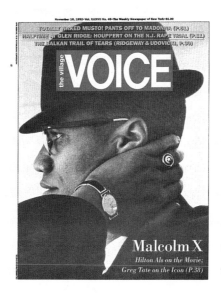

November 16, 1992 • Vol. XXXVII No. 46 • The Weekly Newspaper of New York • $1.00
TOTALLY NAKED MUSTO! PANTS OFF TO MADONNA (P.51)
HALFTIME AT GLEN RIDGE: HOUPPERT ON THE N.J. RAPE TRIAL (P.31)
THE BALKAN TRAIL OF TEARS (RIDGEWAY & UDOVICKI, P.90)

the village VOICE

Malcolm X
Hilton Als on the Movie;
Greg Tate on the Icon (P.38)

Publication The Village Voice
Award Merit
Design Director Robert Newman
Photographer Eve Arnold/Magnum
Photo Editor Tom McGovern
Publisher Village Voice
Publishing Corporation
Category Newspapers/Front Page
Date November 10, 1992

Design

SPREAD

SINGLE PAGE

Redesign

Story

Entire Issue

Information Graphics

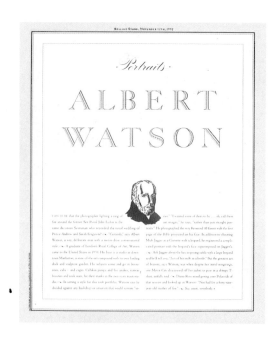

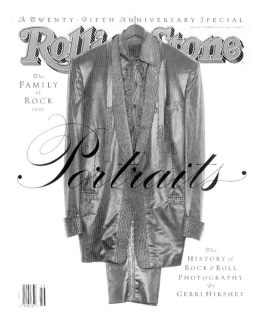

Publication   Rolling Stone
Award   Gold
Art Director   Fred Woodward
Designers   Fred Woodward, Gail Anderson,
     Catherine Gilmore-Barnes,
     Debra Bishop,
     Angela Skouras,
     Geraldine Hessler
Photographers   Albert Watson, Bruce Weber,
     Mark Seliger, Annie Leibovitz,
     Herb Ritts, Kurt Markus
Photo Editor   Laurie Kratochvil
Publisher   Straight Arrow Publishers, Inc.
Category   Design/Entire Issue
Date   November 12, 1992

CARLOS SANTANA

MICK FLEETWOOD & JOHN McVIE

DAVID BYRNE

RAY CHARLES

RICKIE LEE JONES

Publication Dance Ink
Award Gold
Design Director J. Abbott Miller
Designers J. Abbott Miller, Dina Radeka
Photographer Josef Astor
Photo Editor Kate Schlesinger
Publisher Dance Ink, Inc.
Studio Design Writing Research
Category Design/Entire Issue
Date Winter 1992

EYE
WITNESS

ALFRED EISENSTAEDT—born
in Germany in 1898 and still
going strong—is by no means
a dance photographer.
He is a prolific, crackerjack
photojournalist, a mainstay
of *Life* magazine from its
inception, who has specialized in
famous people (portraiture and
candid) and you-are-there takes
on important and interesting
events. His pictures, usually
annotated by his disarming
commentary, have been collected
into several books. Graphically,
these volumes re-create worlds
that, today, seem so near and yet
so far away. While Eisenstaedt's
main occupation has been to
document the people and the
happenings that were the icons
of their time, his love of the
arts has occasionally led him
into enchanting byways.
Two encounters of his camera
with dance subjects, dating from
early in his career, yielded
images of a beauty and a charm
that are hard to resist.

TOBI TOBIAS

Left and above: Paris Opéra, early 1950s

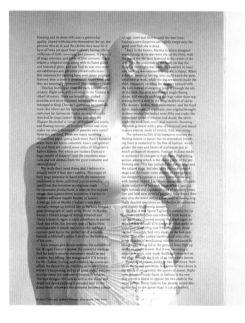

dream
girls
George C. Wolfe's
JELLY'S LAST JAM
is a smooth show
about a mythic music man.

Despite its title, this is not one of those flimsily scripted
revues that hit Broadway so often and so interchange-
ably—a million production numbers in search of a
through-line. *Jelly* is newfangled, an amalgam of *tableaux
vivants*, dramatic lighting effects, and clever framing
devices. Although reminiscent stylistically of Tommy
Tune's *Grand Hotel: The Musical* (and, to a lesser extent,
his earlier *Nine)*, the show also evokes
Les Liaisons Dangereuses (onstage sex),
Cabaret (satanic impresario/host),
and *Once On This Island* (story-theater
devices) without really being as
much like any of them as it is like a
movie. While cinematic approaches
to the stage are nothing new, they
have usually been deconstructions,
reductions, or adaptations of familiar
texts—Peter Brook's *this*, Andrei
Serban's *that*.

Wolfe constructed
JELLY'S LAST JAM
and then directed it.

While conventional wisdom has it that
directing your own play is about as likely to
produce success as conducting your own
psychoanalysis, in this case it couldn't be
any other way. The text—however heartfelt,
sociopolitically correct, and morally driven
("When you get no love, you've got no love
to give")—is an excuse for the visuals.
Robin Wagner has devised settings that echo the structure of Wolfe's scenario—a
series of frames, large and small; some stairs; a ramp (the uphill road to heaven's
gate); some subtle black screens and drops that shape the space.
For almost all the rest, there are people. Wolfe uses his cast—tenderly and lavishly
costumed in remembered colors by Toni-Leslie James—as living scenery. Always,
there is just one picture, and it takes up the entire space available. There's nothing to

NANCY DALVA

Publication Rolling Stone
Award Silver
Art Director Fred Woodward
Designers Fred Woodward, Debra Bishop,
Catherine Gilmore-Barnes,
Gail Anderson,
Angela Skouras,
Geraldine Hessler
Illustrators Barry Blitt, Braldt Bralds,
Steve Brodner, Maris Bishofs,
Charles Burns, Philip Burke,
Steve Calver, Alan E. Cober,
John Collier, Paul Davis,
Rob Day, Blair Drawson,
Regan Dunnick,
Stasys Eidrigevicius,
Mark English, Vivienne Flesher,
Milton Glaser,
Robert Goldstrom, Josh Gosfield,
Alexa Grace, Gottfried Helnwein,
Brad Holland, Gary Kelley,
Anita Kunz, Skip Liepke,
Daniel Maffia, Matt Mahurin,
James McMullan, Bill Nelson,
Michael Paraskevas, C.F. Payne,
Robert Risko, Anthony Russo,
Witkor Sadowski,
Daniel Schwartz, Lane Smith,
Mark Summers, Mark Ulriksen,
Tom Woodruff, Janet Woolley
Photo Editor Laurie Kratochvil
Publisher Straight Arrow Publishers, Inc.
Category Design/Entire Issue
Date October 15, 1992

John Lennon "I like rock & roll, and I don't like much else. It gets through to you."

BY JANN S. WENNER

Bob Dylan "I had a few bands in high school. But lead singers would always come in and take my bands because their fathers would have connections, so they could get a job in the next town at a Sunday picnic. And I'd lose my band. I'd see it all the time."

BY KURT LODER

Little Richard "I have seen people foaming at the mouth and just wanting to touch me."

BY PARKE PUTERBAUGH

WoRld ToUR

A REVIEW OF WORLDWIDE BUSINESS AND TECHNOLOGY NEWS PUBLISHED BY DUN & BRADSTREET SOFTWARE   VOLUME 2 NO. 1 MARCH 1992

All these people have something in common. Charles Babbage 50 Isambard Brunel 48 Chester Carlson 7 Rachel Carson 46 Confucius INSERT Nicholas Copernicus 64 Loring Crosman 29 Leonardo da Vinci INSERT Charles Darwin 42 Miles Davis 60 Simone de Beauvoir 106 Franz Fanon 106 Hugh Ferriss 85 Buckminster Fuller 91 Mahatma Gandhi 66 Joseph Glidden 89 Robert Goddard 25 Hesiod 105 Soichiro Honda 58 Raymond Hood 85 George Jenks 108 Carl Jung 62 August Kekulé 54 John Maynard Keynes 105 Charlie Klemt 21 George McGill 1 Henry Miller 38 Samuel Morse 37 Isamu Noguchi 5 Brian O'Leary 22 Gerard O'Neill 22 Donald Partridge 81 Louis Pasteur 44 Albert Pratt 33 Pierre Proudhon 104 Edwin Pynchon 99 Adam Smith 105 Robert Smithson 11 Laurence Sterne 106 Nikola Tesla 40 Frank Vester 73 Andy Warhol 52 Howard Wheeler 69 Virginia Woolf 56 They're of the same mold, because what they set out to do was shatter the mold. They had the ability to break entrenched thought patterns in their fields, and in so doing some of them irrevocably changed the world. This issue of *World Tour* celebrates the act of change, sometimes called re-engineering or paradigm shifting. It's dedicated to people like these, who whether they succeed or fail, pursue visions that are often called chimeras in their generation, and reality in the next. **Technology** Anti-noise 8 Artificial Islands 31 Asian TV 9 Biomass 16 Biomimicry 18 Biotechnology 10 Cartography 20 CDs 8 Computer-Aided Surgery 24 Computerized Gorilla Speech 12 DAT 36 Drug Design 26 EC Nervous System 24 Electric Cars 20 Electronic Democracy 10 Electronic Vaults 31 Eye Tracking 13 Face Interface 13 Fusion 17 Gadget Gap 26 HDTV 23 MOT Degree 24 Multimedia 10 Neural Networks 18 New Developments 6 Notebook Peripherals 18 Nuclear Power 17 Object-Oriented Programming 26 Oil 16 Patents 36 Pattern Recognition 9 Pen-Based Computers 12 Personal Communications 36 Privacy 28 Solar Fuel 16 Tech Trends 23 Teraflops 13 Turing Test 23 Wearable Computers 12 Wireless LANs 8 World Brain 9 **Business** Anger 79 Arms Control 101 Books 104 Capitalism 68 Corporate Espionage 101 Cuba 92 Czechoslovakia 92 Deadhead Quality 70 Deming 71 Denmark 92 Education 98 Former USSR 90 France 92 Germany 92 Global Recession 87 Great Britain 93 Green Economy 72 Hostile Takeovers 96 Hype 79 Japan 82 Korea 93 Learning Organizations 78 Maastricht 84 Marx 80 Mexico 93 Mittelstand 83 Mommy Track 78 Network Management 68 New Media 80 Offices 97 Outsourcing 72 Ozone Hole 84 Poetry 101 Populism 72 Racism 86 Self-Managed IS Teams 96 Separatism 88 Sexual Harassment 100 Spain 93 Stress 79 Total Quality 70 Tribal Knowledge 88 United States 93 Videoconferencing 96 Waste 100 Work 78 Working Smarter 97

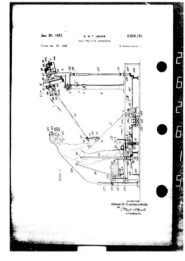

Publication	World Tour
Award	Silver
Design Director	Gary Koepke
Art Director	Gary Koepke
Designer	Diddo Ramm
Studio	Koepke Design Group
Category	Design/Entire Issue
Date	March 1992

Publication	Mohawk Paper Promotion
Award	Silver
Design Director	Michael Bierut
Designers	Michael Bierut, Lisa Cerveny, Dana Arnett, P. Scott Makela
Photographers	Francois Robert, Tom Strong, John Paul Endress
Studio	Pentagram Design
Client	Mohawk Paper Mills
Category	Design/Entire Issue
Date	Fall 1992

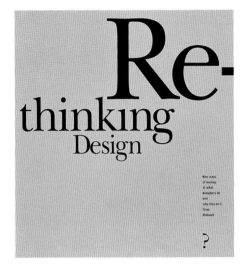

Re-thinking Design

New ways of looking at what designers do and why they do it. From Mohawk.

?

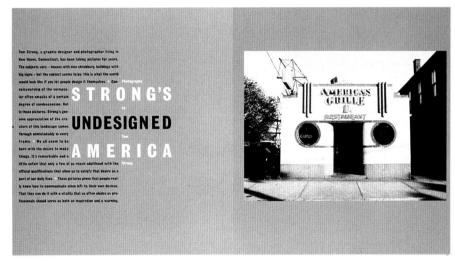

Larry Keeley is interested in what *confuses*, *delights* or *upsets* people. But what does that stuff have to do with *design*?

An interview with Doblin Group President Larry Keeley by Janet Abrams Photography by Francois Robert

Photography STRONG'S by UNDESIGNED Tom AMERICA Strong

AMERICA'S GRILLE RESTAURANT

JustSayNo

Photography by John Paul Endress

Publication	Rolling Stone
Award	Merit
Art Director	Fred Woodward
Designers	Fred Woodward, Debra Bishop, Catherine Gilmore-Barnes, Gail Anderson, Angela Skouras, Geraldine Hessler
Illustrators	Dennis Ortiz-Lopez, Brian Cronin, Ralph Staedman, Jamie Putnam, Matt Mahurin, Henrik Drescher
Photographers	Annie Leibovitz, Arthur H. Gorson, Max Aguilera-Hellweg, Mary Ellen Mark, Alfred Werthimer, Hiro, Bonnie Schiffman, David Katzenstein, Herb Ritts/Visages
Photo Editor	Laurie Kratochvil
Publisher	Straight Arrow Publishers, Inc.
Category	Design/Entire Issue
Date	June 11, 1992

By Chet Flippo

DOLLY PARTON

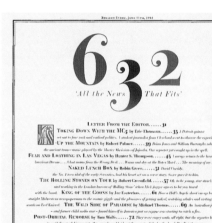

By David Black

The Plague Years

Publication	American Photo
Award	Merit
Art Director	Mark Gartland
Designer	Patricia Marroquin
Photographers	Matthew Rolston, Horst
Publisher	Hachette Magazines, Inc.
Category	Design/Entire Issue
Date	January/February 1992

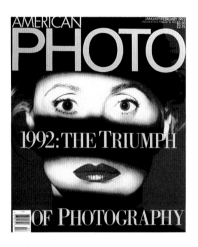

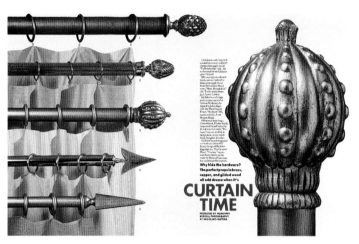

Publication	Elle Decor
Award	Merit
Art Director	Caroline Bowyer
Designers	Jo Hay, Caroline Bowyer
Photographer	Ned Matura
Publisher	Hachette Magazines, Inc.
Category	Design/Entire Issue
Date	June/July 1992

Publication	Entertainment Weekly
Award	Merit
Design Director	Michael Grossman
Art Director	Mark Michaelson
Designers	Michael Grossman, Mark Michaelson, Miriam Campiz
Photo Editor	Mary Dunn, Anastasia Pleasant
Publisher	Entertainment Weekly, Inc.
Date	January 10, 1992

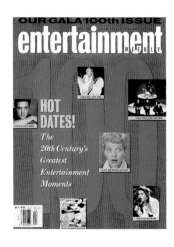

Publication	Entertainment Weekly
Award	Merit
Design Director	Michael Grossman
Art Director	Mark Michaelson
Designers	Michael Grossman, Mark Michaelson, Elizabeth Betts, Jeff Christensen
Illustrators	Josh Gosfield, Nola Lopez, Drew Friedman, Steve Meyers, Hanoch Piven, Grace Knott, Steve Cerio, Lisa Adams, Scott Gillis, Barry Blitt
Photographers	Hiro , Brigitte Lacombe, Theo Westenberger, Gregory Heisler, James Schnept, Sylvia Otte, Wayne Maser, Roven Afanador, Corrine Day, Jeffery Newbury, Herb Ritts, Eika Aoshima
Photo Editors	Mary Dunn, Mark Jacobson
Publisher	Entertainment Weekly, Inc.
Category	Design/Entire Issue
Date	December 25, 1992

Perfection!

Publication Harper's Bazaar
Award Merit
Creative Director Fabien Baron
Art Director Joel Berg
Designer Johan Svensson
Photographers Patrick Demarchelier, Peter Lindbergh,
Mario Testino, Paul Warchol
Publisher The Hearst Corporation
Category Design/Entire Issue
Date December 1992

CLEAN CUT
THE ENDURING APPEAL
OF RESORT: AZURE WATER,
SUN-KISSED SKIN, SENSUAL
CLOTHES THAT DEFINE
THE BODY IN GRAPHIC
BLACK AND WHITE

PHOTOGRAPHED BY PATRICK DEMARCHELIER

Casual chic: Black matte jersey sleeveless jumpsuit with wide legs and cutout back by Donna Karan. Sunglasses, Optical Affairs by Christian Roth.

Diamonds
may be forever, but the way they're
worn is not. Instead of being a means to
dazzle, they're now a more private pleasure worn
with the same comfort, the same easy familiarity, as a
favorite sweater. Opposite page: Ring with a center oval canary
diamond and round diamonds at the sides, from Van Cleef & Arpels.
Gray wool turtleneck, about $350, from Paul Smith. This page: Ring with a
center oval diamond set in platinum with triangular side diamonds, from Harry Winston.

Publication Hemispheres
Award Merit
Design Director Kit Hinrichs
Art Directors Kit Hinrichs, Jamiey Easler
Designer Jackie Foshaug
Illustrator Ikko Tanaka
Publisher Pace Communications
Studio Pentagram Design
Client United Airlines
Category Design/Entire Issue
Date October 1992

Publication Harper's Bazaar
Award Merit
Creative Director Fabien Baron
Art Director Joel Berg
Designer Johan Svensson
Photographers Patrick Demarchelier,
Peter Lindbergh,
Mario Testino, Paul Warchol,
Michel Arnaud
Publisher The Hearst Corporation
Category Design/Entire Issue
Date September 1992

Publication Martha Stewart Living
Award Merit
Design Director Gail Towey
Art Director Gail Towey
Designers Jennifer Waerek, Laura Harigan, Ann Johnson
Photographers Victoria Pearson, Davies & Starr, Ruven Afanador
Publisher Time Publishing Ventures
Category Design/Entire Issue
Date October/November 1992

Publication Men's Journal
Award Merit
Art Director Matthew Drace
Designers Giovanni Russo, Gaemer Gutierrez
Ilustrators C.F. Payne, Roxanna Villa
Photographers George Holz, Neal Rogers
Publisher Straight Arrow Publishers
Category Design/Entire Issue
Date November/December 1992

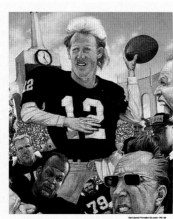

Publication	Life
Award	Merit
Design Director	Tom Bentkowski
Art Director	Nora Sheehan
Designer	Nora Sheehan
Photographer	Lynn Johnson
Photo Editor	Barbara Baker Burrows
Publisher	Time/Warner, Inc.
Category	Design/Entire Issue
Date	June 1992

Publication	North Carolina Literary Review
Award	Merit
Design Directors	Alex Albright, Eva Roberts
Art Director	Eva Roberts
Designers	Eva Roberts, Curt Wommack
Illustrators	Stanton Blakeslee, Andy Sugg
Photo Editor	Alex Albright
Publisher	East Carolina University, Greenville, NC
Client	English Department, East Carolina University
Category	Design/Entire Issue
Date	Summer 1992

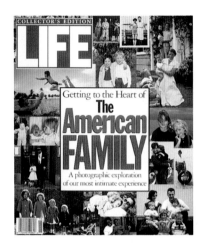

Publication Computer Reseller News
Award Merit
Art Director Gene Fedele
Designers Steve Merin, Tami Zipser, Dave Nicastro
Publisher CMP Publications
Category Design/Entire Issue
Date June 1992

Publication Architectural Record
Award Merit
Design Director Alberto Bucchianeri
Designers Alberto Bucchianeri, Anna Egger -Schlesinger
Publisher McGraw-Hill Publications
Category Design/Entire Issue
Date May 1992

Publication	Glass
Award	Merit
Design Director	Michael Bierut
Designers	Michael Bierut, Kevin Lauterback
Photographer	Robert Mapplethorpe
Studio	Pentagram Design, NY
Client	New York Experimental Glass Workshop
Category	Design/Entire Issue
Date	Winter 1992

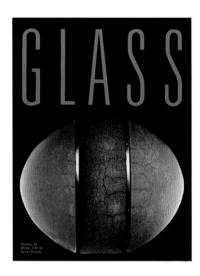

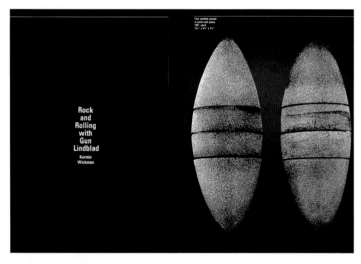

Publication	Forbes FYI
Award	Merit
Art Director	Alexander Isley
Designer	Lynette Cortez
Illustrator	Paul Cox
Publisher	Forbes, Inc.
Studio	Alexander Isley Design
Category	Design/Entire Issue
Date	November 1992

Publication	P4 Magazine
Award	Merit
Design Director	John Rushworth
Art Director	John Rushworth
Designers	Vince Frost, John Rushworth
Photographers	The Douglas Brothers, Giles Perrin
Photo Editor	The Douglas Brothers
Publisher	Polaroid UK
Studio	Pentagram Design Ltd.
Client	Polaroid
Category	Design/Entire Issue
Date	February 1992

Publication	U&lc
Award	Merit
Design Director	Milton Glaser
Art Directors	Walter Bernard, Milton Glaser
Designers	Frank Baseman, Sharon Okamoto
Publisher	International Typeface Corp.
Studio	WBMG, Inc.
Category	Design/Entire Issue
Date	Spring 1992

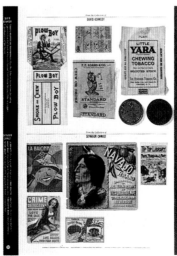

Publication Digital News
Award Merit
Design Director Mark Koudys
Designer Mark Koudys
Photographer Ron Baker Smith
Studio Atlanta Art and Design, Toronto
Category Design/Entire Issue
Date November 1992

Quality of
Life

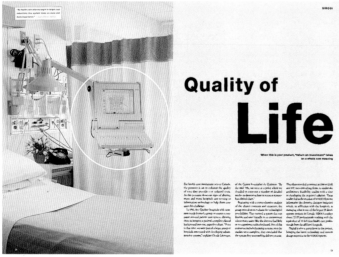

Publication Digital News
Award Merit
Design Director Mark Koudys
Designer Mark Koudys
Photographer Ron Baker Smith
Studio Atlanta Art and Design, Toronto
Category Design/Entire Issue
Date August 1992

Publication Here & Now
Award Merit
Design Directors John Hornall, Julia LaPine
Art Directors John Hornall, Julia LaPine
Designers John Hornall, Julia LaPine, Heidi Hatlestad, David Bates, Bruce Branson-Meyer, Lian Ng
Illustrator Dan Picasso
Photographer Rosanne Olson
Studio Hornall Anderson Design Works, Inc.
Client Comprehensive Health Education Foundation
Category Design/Entire Issue
Date September 1992

Métro métro / Les deux sont le Métro / Mais s le cinéma a un lion

— Le cinéma Metro que je connais depuis toujo ours, le "Metro" de mon enfance.
— Au début des gens pensaient que le M d qu nou-veau métro souterrain était l'initiale de Moubarak... Pourquoi l'appelle-t-on métro en arabe ? Et t pour-quoi le cinéma Metro ?
— Les premières semaines, dans le métro du Caire les voyageurs avaient l'air intimidé. Je me souvien d'une famille avec de beaux habits — c'était en novembre 1987, juste après l'inauguration. Les deux petites filles avaient des nœuds dans les cheveux et des chaussettes blanches. Leur mère veillait à ce qu'elles ne salissent pas la banquette avec leurs chaussures. Elles parlaient à voix x basse.

— Je me souviens de l'époque où il y avait des poinçonneurs dans le métro pari-sien. Et de la première fois où je l'ai pris. J'étais perdue, mais l'amie avec qui voyageais, elle, elle avait compris qu'il fallait connaître les directions. classique c'était le cinéma Metro et les not drugs chez "Bambou", un peu plus loin, sur le même trottoir. En ce temps ils mettaient du beurre et de la moutarde, c'étaient des petits ins qu'on ne trouvait pas partout. près on traversait et on allait là avec le sirop rouge et les morceaux de arrons glacés, dans un petit bol en métal.
uand j'avais douze ans, chaque ven-dredi au Metro il y avait ciné-club. Ma sœur aînée y allait. Elle a vu les plus beaux films que moi je n'ai jamais vus jusqu'à aujourd'hui ; Vadim... Truffaut....

Publication Irregulomadaire
Award Merit
Design Directors Susanna Shannon, Jérôme Saint-Loubert Bié, Jean-Charles Depaule
Art Director Jérôme Oudin
Designers Jean-Charles Depaule, Jérome Oudin, Jérôme Saint-Loubert Bié, Suzanna Shannon
Photographer Jérôme Saint-Loubert Bié
Photo Editor Jérôme Saint-Loubert Bié
Publisher Irregulomadaire
Client Irregulomadaire
Category Design/Entire Issue
Date Summer 1992

Publication	Lear's "Connection" Newsletter
Award	Merit
Design Director	Bruce Ramsay
Art Director	Paula Kelly
Photo Editor	Paula Kelly
Publisher	Lear's Publishing
Category	Design/Entire Issue
Date	Vol. 1, No. 4 1992

Publication	Lear's "Connection" Newsletter
Award	Merit
Design Directors	Bruce Ramsay, Paula Kelly
Art Director	Paula Kelly
Designer	Paula Kelly
Photo Editor	Paula Kelly
Publisher	Lear's Publishing
Category	Design/Entire Issue
Date	Vol. 1, No. 2 1992

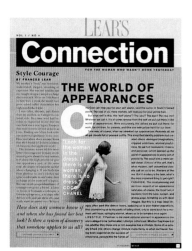

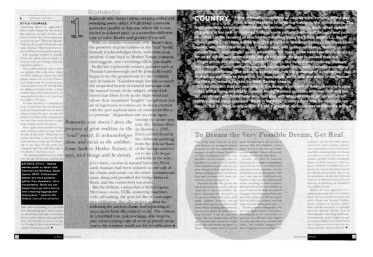

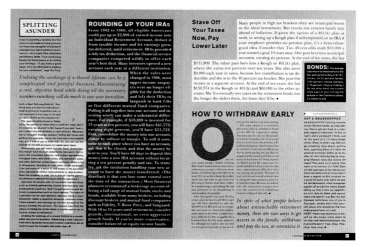

Publication Lida Baday Brochure
Award Merit
Art Directors Diti Katona, John Pylypczak
Designer Diti Katona
Photographer Karen Levy
Studio Concrete Design Communications Inc.
Category Design/Entire Issue
Date 1992

Publication Lyric Opera Brochure
Award Merit
Design Director John Muller
Art Director John Muller
Designers John Muller, Scott Chapman
Photographer Mike Regnier
Photo Editor John Muller
Studio Muller + Company
Client The Kansas City Lyric Opera
Category Design/Entire Issue
Date 1992

Publication Show Offs
Award Merit
Art Directors Jan Ellis, Laurie Ellis
Designers Jan Ellis, Laurie Ellis
Photographer Mark Tucker
Studio Ellis Design
Client Athens Paper
Category Design/Entire Issue
Date July 1992

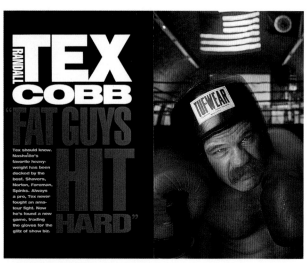

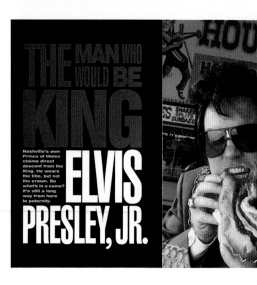

Publication Otis School of Art and Design
Award Merit
Art Directors Michael Hodgson, Clive Piercy
Designers Michael Hodgson, Clive Piercy, Denise Crisp, Carol Kono
Photographer John Reed Forsman
Photo Editor Carol Kono
Studio Ph.D
Client Otis School of Art and Design
Category Design/Entire Issue
Date 1992

Publication Signatures of the Body
Award Merit
Design Director Susan Hochbaum
Art Director Susan Hochbaum
Designer Susan Hochbaum
Illustrators Steven Guarnaccia, Richard McGuire
Photographer Sandi Fellman
Publisher Mead Paper
Studio Pentagram Design, NYC
Client Mead Paper
Category Design/Entire Issue
Date March 1992

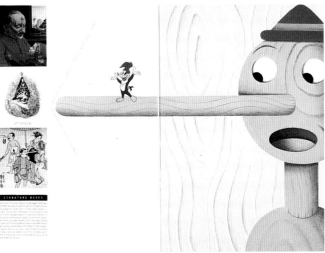

Publication Subjective Reasoning 3
Award Merit
Design Directors Paula Scher, Bill Drenttel
Designer Duane Michals
Photographer Duane Michals
Publisher Champion International
Studio Pentagram Design, NYC
Client Champion International
Category Design/Entire Issue
Date October 1992

Publication	Subjective Reasoning 2
Award	Merit
Design Directors	Paula Scher, Bill Drentel
Art Director	Paula Scher
Designer	Paula Scher
Illustrator	Paula Scher
Publisher	Champion International
Studio	Pentagram/Drentell Doyle
Client	Champion International
Category	Design/Entire Issue
Date	September 1992

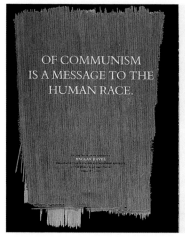

It is a message we have not yet fully deciphered and comprehended. In its deepest sense, the end of Communism has brought a major era in human history to an end. It has brought an end not just to the 19th and 20th centuries, but to the modern age as a whole.

The modern era has been dominated by the culminating belief, expressed in different forms, that the world—and Being as such—is a wholly knowable system governed by a finite number of universal laws that man can grasp and rationally direct for his own benefit. This era, beginning in the Renaissance and developing from the Enlightenment to socialism, from positivism to scientism, from the Industrial Revolution to the information revolution, was characterized by rapid advances in rational, cognitive thinking.

This, in turn, gave rise to the proud belief that man, as the pinnacle of everything that exists, was capable of objectively describing, explaining and controlling everything that exists, and of possessing the one and only truth about the world. It was an era in which there was a cult of depersonalized objectivity, an era in which objective knowledge was amassed and technologically exploited, an era of belief in automatic progress brokered by the scientific method. It was an era of systems, institutions, mechanisms and statistical averages. It was an era of ideologies, doctrines, interpretations of reality, an era in which the goal was to find a universal theory of the world, and thus a universal

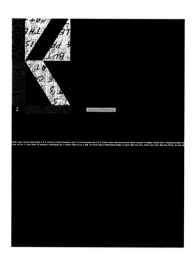

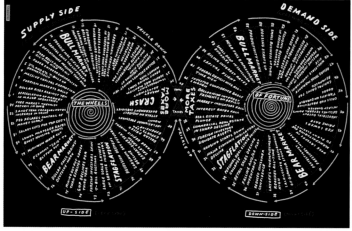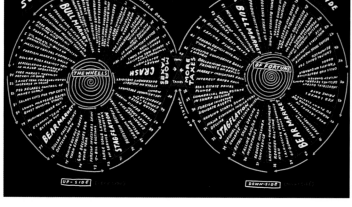

The single biggest ecological issue is acid-rain. The single biggest ecological crisis is the disappearance of the rain-forest. The single biggest obligation of the environmental movement is to educate people about the consequences of "convenience." The single most urgent ecological issue is eradicating fossil-fuels. The single most important ecological issue is saving the oceans. The single most explosive environmental issue is nuclear technology. The single most urgent environmental need is the development of alternative fuels.

Publication	Subjective Reasoning 1
Award	Merit
Design Directors	Paula Scher, Bill Drenttel
Art Director	Stephen Doyle
Designer	Stephen Doyle
Illustrator	Stephen Doyle
Publisher	Champion International
Studio	Pentagram Design/Drenttel Doyle
Client	Champion International
Category	Design/Entire Issue
Date	July 1992

WoRld ToUR

ЗДРАВСТВУЙТЕ, ПРИВЕТСТВУЮ ВАС!

祝 你们大家好

สวัสดีค่ะ สหายในธรณีใหม่ พวกเราในธรณีนี้ขอส่งมิตรจิตมาถึงท่านทุกคน

हम धरती के निवासी आप का स्वागत करते हैं।

ಕನ್ನಡಿಗರ ಪರವಾಗಿ ಶುಭಾಶಯಂಗಳು

各位好嗎? 祝各位平安健康快樂.

안 녕 하 세 요 ?

पृथ्वीवासीहरूद्वारा भ्रान्तिमय भविष्यको शुभकामना !

LEAVE YOUR ORDER HERE.

Publication World Tour
Award Merit
Design Director Gary Koepke
Art Director Gary Koepke
Designer Diddo Ramm
Studio Koepke Design Group
Category Design/Entire Issue
Date July 1992

monitor

quick

Publication Zapata Brochure
Award Merit
Art Directors John Pylpczak, Diti Katona
Designer Diti Katona
Photographer Deborah Samuel
Studio Concrete Design Communications, Inc.
Category Design/Entire Issue
Date 1992

Spring 93

Contact: Gangbar Winslade 57 Spadina Ave. Suite 213 Toronto Ontario CAN. M5V 2J2 (416)340-0455 Zapata 1290 Bay St. Toronto Ontario CAN M5R 2C3 (416) 924 5744 Credits: make-up & hair: Rena Andreoli Model: Marguerite Merkly Stylist: Barbara Waltman Graphic Design: Diti Katona Concrete Toronto Photography: Deborah Samuel L.A.

Publication	Zoo Views
Award	Merit
Design Director	Melanie Doherty
Designers	Melanie Doherty, Joan Folkmann
Photographer	Steve Underwood
Photo Editor	Melanie Doherty
Studio	Melanie Doherty Design
Client	San Francisco Zoological Society
Category	Design/Entire Issue
Date	January/February 1992

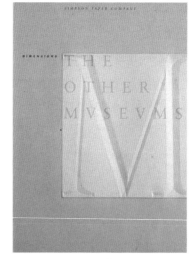

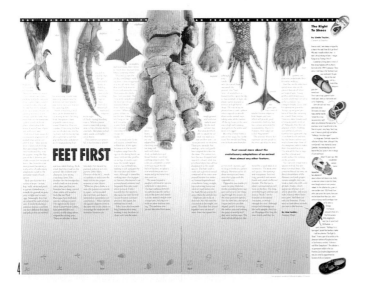

Publication	Dimensions 1992
Award	Merit
Design Director	Richard Poulin
Art Director	Richard Poulin
Designers	Richard Poulin, Rosemary Simpkins
Publisher	Simpson Paper Company
Studio	Richard Poulin Design Group Inc.
Client	Simpson Paper Company
Category	Design/Entire Issue
Date	May 1992

Publication Corrections Corporation of America Annual Report
Award Merit
Design Director Laurie Ellis
Art Directors Jan Ellis, Laurie Ellis
Designers Jan Ellis, Laurie Ellis
Photographer Mark Tucker
Studio Ellis Design
Client Corrections Corporation
Category Design/Entire Issue
Date 1992

Publication Community Partnership of Santa Clara County
Annual Report
Award Merit
Art Directors Earl Gee, Fani Chung
Designers Earl Gee, Fani Chung
Illustrator Earl Gee
Studio Earl Gee Design
Client Community Partnership of Santa Clara County
Category Design/Entire Issue
Date September 1992

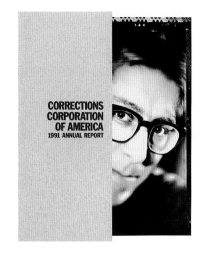

CORRECTIONS CORPORATION OF AMERICA
1991 ANNUAL REPORT

THE FIRST YEAR

Building *the* **PARTNERSHIP**

DEWITT BLOUNT
VENUS PRE-RELEASE CENTER

QUESTIONS:

an actual

WORKING

organization?

DESSIE BACA
NEW MEXICO WOMEN'S CORRECTIONAL FACILITY

Publication	Kaplan Rules Cards
Award	Merit
Design Director	John Parham
Art Director	Rick Stermole
Photographers	Miranda Turin, Nick Basilion
Studio	Parham-Santana Inc.
Client	Stanley H. Kaplan Educational Center LTD.
Category	Design/Entire Issue
Date	1992

Publication	Time Warner Inc. 1992 Annual Report
Award	Merit
Creative Director	Kent Hunter
Design Director	Aubrey Balkind
Designers	Ruth Diener, Kent Hunter
Illustrators	Josh Gosfield, J.D. King
Studio	Frankfurt Gips Balkind
Client	Time Warner Inc.
Category	Design/Entire Issue
Date	May 1992

Meet the inventor of test prep. Our most venerable **founder**. Stanley H. Kaplan, the original whiz kid, the first and only true braintrainer. Stanley may not wear the latest hightops and we've never seen him in baggies. But when it comes to tests, Stanley knows how to score. Stanley, like all true brains, believes that there's no substitute for actual knowledge. For real instruction. For deep strategy. For more than 50 years, Stanley and his in-the-trenches teachers have raised scores. Stanley may have taught your mother. Stanley has stood behind over 2 million students — more than all other test preppers, combined! Come in and catch the Stanley spirit of test prep. Train your brain.

Truth is you can reach a **higher** score. Kaplan SAT students go up — **substantially** — and are in a stronger position for making the college of their choice. This jump is measured by comparing your score before you come to Kaplan to your post-Kaplan score on the actual SAT.

Get real. Say good-bye to the myth that the SAT is a terror test devised by braingods who live in remote regions of Academia. The SAT is a fairly predictable test devised by ordinary people who work out of a suburb in New Jersey. You can learn how to master it.

Confident
Open the test, there are no surprises. You already know the test instructions. You already know how to pace yourself. You already know what to expect in every section of the test, because you've encountered it before, lots of times: in the classroom, during our practice tests, and with the instructors. Kaplan gives you real instruction and real results.

Publication San Francisco International Airport
Award Merit
Design Director Jennifer Morla
Art Director Jennifer Morla
Designers Jennifer Morla, Sharrie Brooks
Photographer Art Lab, Inc.
Studio Morla Design
Client San Francisco International Airport
Category Design/Entire Issue
Date October 1992

Publication VH1 Capabilities Brochure
Award Merit
Design Director Cheri Dorr
Art Director Okey Nestor
Studio Parham-Santana Inc.
Client VH1 Channel (MTV Networks)
Category Design/Entire Issue
Date 1992

San Francisco International Airport introduced service abroad with the first West Coast flight to Asia. The *1992 Annual Report* is presented during a period of continued rapid growth in international service. Two hundred twenty-four flights weekly provide convenient non-stop service to twenty destinations worldwide.

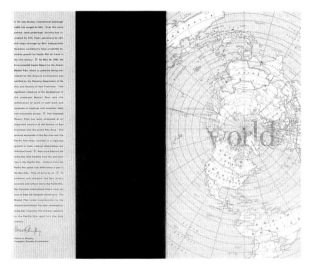

Publication LA Weekly
Award Merit
Art Directors Scott Ford, Bill Smith
Designers Laura Steele, David Goldman, Robin Ogata
Illustrator Rick Morris
Photo Editor Howard Rosenberg
Publisher LA Weekly
Category Design/Entire Issue
Date September 25, 1992

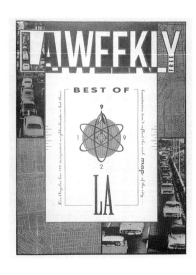

Publication The New York Times/Styles
Award Merit
Art Director Ken McFarlin
Designer Ken McFarlin
Photographer Naum Kazhdan
Publisher The New York Times
Category Design/Entire Issue
Date November 8, 1992

Publication SPY
Award Merit
Art Director Christiaan Kuypers
Designers David Vogler, Damon Torres, Daniel Carter
Illustrators Daniel Carter, Gregg Trueman
Photo Editor Nicki Gostin
Publisher SPY Corporation
Category Design/Entire Issue
Date July 1992

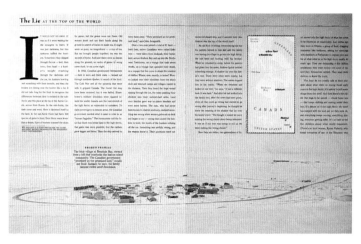

Publication The Boston Globe Magazine
Award Merit
Art Director Lucy Bartholomay
Designer Lucy Bartholomay
Photographer Michele McDonald
Photo Editor Lucy Bartholomay
Publisher The Boston Globe Publishing Co.
Category Design/Entire Issue
Date August 9, 1992

Publication The Boston Globe/Special Section
Award Merit
Art Director Rena Sokolow
Designer Rena Sokolow
Illustrators Ward Shumaker, Anthony Russo
Photo Editor Jacqueline Berthet
Publisher The Boston Globe Publishing Co.
Category Design/Entire Issue
Date March 29, 1992

Publication The Boston Globe
Award Merit
Design Director Aldona Charlton
Art Director Aldona Charlton
Designer Aldona Charlton
Illustrators Dave Brady, Warren Linn, Federico Botana
Photo Editor Aldona Charlton
Publisher The Boston Globe Publishing Co.
Category Design/Entire Issue
Date October 25, 1992

Publication Hat Life Directory
Award Merit
Art Director Alex Bonziglia
Designer Alex Bonziglia
Photographer Scott Wippermann
Studio David Morris Design Associates
Category Design/Entire Issue
Date 1992

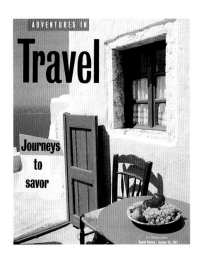

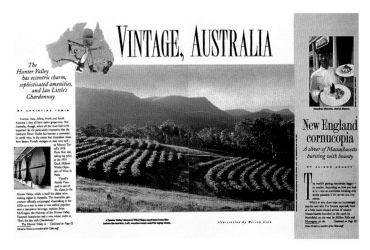

Publication The Boston Globe/Special Section
Award Merit
Design Director Lynn Staley
Designers Lynn Staley, Rena Sokolow
Publisher The Boston Globe Publishing Co.
Category Design/Entire Issue
Date July 5, 1992

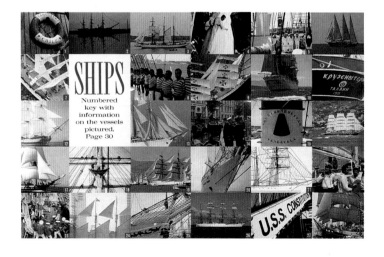

Publication The New York Times Magazine
Award Merit
Design Director Tom Bodkin
Art Director Janet Froelich
Designer Janet Froelich
Photographers Duane Michals, Keith Carter, Norman Watson
Publisher The New York Times
Category Design/Entire Issue
Date September 13, 1992

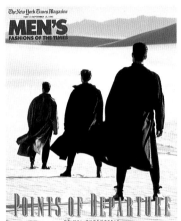

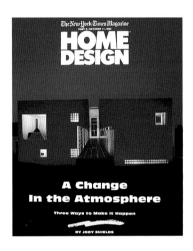

Publication The New York Times Magazine
Award Merit
Design Director Tom Bodkin
Art Director Linda Brewer
Designer Linda Brewer
Photographer James Wojcik
Publisher The New York Times
Category Design/Entire Issue
Date October 11, 1992

Publication Harper's Bazaar
Award Gold
Creative Director Fabien Baron
Art Director Joel Berg
Designer Johan Svensson
Photographers Patrick Demarchelier,
Peter Lindbergh
Publisher The Hearst Corporation
Category Design/Redesign
Date September 1992

For thousands of years we've been decorating our faces. But why? Tina Gaudoin debates the politics of

MAKE UP

Never mind the adage men don't cry. In this culture (by and large), men don't wear makeup. Elementary? Well, think about it. In 1991 American women spent $4.7 billion on maquillage and millions of hours on the choice of products and their application. For most of us, that's probably dollars and time well spent. Nonetheless, it begs the question: Why, and for whom? Is makeup part of our mating ritual? A pleasure enhancer? Or is it our protection (physically and metaphorically) against the outside world? Do we wear it for ourselves or for others? And, perhaps most important, are we in danger of becoming makeup-dependent?

"If we did away with the cosmetics companies and advertising completely, women would reinvent the industry. Making up is quite literally in our genes; it's part of our genetic reproductive strategy," says Helen Fisher, Ph.D., an anthropologist at the American Museum of Natural

Q
fall's refined appeal

uiet luxury, considered fine, beautiful fabrics: These are the qualities that epitomize the new elegance that underlies fall's flashier changes. These are clothes beyond the seasonal vagaries of fashion, yet within their timeless appeal show real, substantive changes that are absolutely of the moment. A sweeping black evening dress that bares only the shoulders in a statement of subtle exposure. A soft gray cashmere worn with matching trousers, in a completely original variation on the suit. "Elegance is understatement," says Calvin Klein. "The woman should stand out; the clothes should not overtake her." There's an integrity of design that allows these pieces to stand on their own: They don't need the glittery camouflage of a wristful of bracelets or strands of necklaces to look finished. "That ethic of jeweled, fussy, scalloped, and teased is just not in my world anymore," says Isaac Mizrahi. "Now a scent, a defined eyebrow, is all you need." Impeccable in balance, cut, and proportion, these are the clothes that, by virtue of their practicality, their lack of pretension, are the foundation of a great wardrobe. A new generation comes to evening. Opposite page: Black viscose/Lycra turtleneck, drop-waist dress, about $1375, by Donna Karan.

The sensuality of leather against skin. Opposite page: Coat with shearling collar and cuffs by Gianni Versace. Eric Javits hat. The new evening paradigm of black and bare. This page: Vest with wool jersey back, about $410, and mid-calf skirt, about $510, both by Jennifer George.

BLACK leather

Motorcycle mania brought black leather as much into the fashion vernacular as the little black dress. While the trend made us more comfortable wearing what had always been considered the outward manifestation of a dangerous mind, the fascination quickly degenerated when a flock of Perfecto-wearing poseurs turned the biker jacket into something so routine, so overworked, that all its original seduction and rebellion wore bad. This fall, designers rescue black leather from the tired Hell's Angels idiom. It shows up everywhere with a chic new edge, in forms that are wearable, diverse, and anything but commonplace. Quilted pants. Sculpted jackets. Long slit skirts banded with white. What's also different is that these new pieces are not confined to one look, or one context: Now leather pants work in the office, worn with a white shirt. Black leather will given a feeling of protection, of invincibility, but its connotations have changed from sinister to sexy. In times like these, it can't hurt to don a literal thick skin. The new artistry in black leather. Opposite page: Fitted jacket, about $3785, quilted pants, about $1035, and combat boots, about $1045, all by Karl Lagerfeld for Chanel.

The sixth goes luxe in leather. Opposite page: Long trench, about $2460, Anne Klein Collection by Louis Dell'Olio. The reptilish trim is a dry counterpoint to slick black. This page: patent-brocaded jacket with white stitching, about $4135, white wide-collar crepe bodysuit, about $955, and silk tie, all by Karl Lagerfeld. Hat, Dolce & Gabbana.

Publication Discover
Award Merit
Art Director David Armario
Designer David Armario
Illustrator Malcolm Tarlofsky
Photographers Gregory Heisler, Max Aguillera-Hellweg, Davies & Starr
Photo Editor John Barker
Publisher Disney Magazine Publishing
Category Design/Redesign
Date September 1992

Publication	Garbage
Award	Merit
Design Director	Patrick Mitchell
Designer	Patrick Mitchell
Illustrators	Chad Draper, Steve Pietzsch, Gary Tanhauser, Brian Smale, Scott Morgan
Photographers	David Wharton, Brian Smale
Publisher	Dovetale Publishers
Category	Design/Redesign
Date	December/January 1993

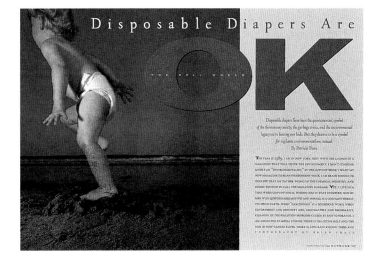

Publication	Hemispheres
Award	Merit
Design Director	Kit Hinrichs
Art Directors	Kit Hinrichs, Jamiey Easler
Designer	Jackie Foshaug
Illustrator	Ikko Tanaka
Publisher	Pace Communications
Studio	Pentagram Design
Client	United Airlines
Category	Design/Redesign
Date	October 1992

Publication Life in Medicine
Award Merit
Design Director Sara Giovanitti
Art Director Gail M. Kamenish
Designer Sara Giovanitti
Illustrators Philippe Weisbecker, Vivienne Flesher,
Judy Pedersen
Publisher Physician Services of America
Category Design/Redesign

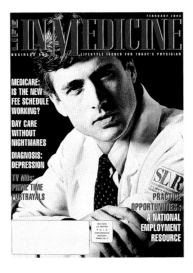

Publication Magazine Week
Award Merit
Design Directors Milton Glaser, Walter Bernard
Designers Frank Baseman, Sharon Okamoto,
Charles Dixon III
Photographer Albert Watson
Publisher Magazine Week, Inc.
Studio WBMG, Inc.
Category Design/Redesign
Date October 19, 1992

OCTOBER 19, 1992   THE NEWSWEEKLY OF MAGAZINE PUBLISHING   NUMBER 334

FIRST PICK

An Old Feud Heats Up...

Rolling Stone October 29: The dread Sinead sans props by Albert Watson. See page 3.

IRIS COHEN SELINGER

No one would ever say Steve Florio is shy. Adjacent to his handsome, very cherry wood office at *The New Yorker* is his shrine — a private bathroom lined with photographs and framed newspaper articles of his successes. In fact, within the corridors of Conde Nast, Florio's self-promotion is sometimes jokingly compared to Don King's.

But the *New Yorker* president hardly corners the prima donna market at Conde Nast.

(Continued on page 21)

Publication Person to Person
Award Merit
Design Director Robert Petrick
Art Director Robert Petrick
Designers Robert Petrick, Laura Ress
Photo Editor Laura Ress
Studio Petrick Design
Client Foote, Cone, & Belding
Category Design/Redesign
Date Vol. 10, No. 1, November 1992

Publication	Harper's Bazaar
Award	Gold
Creative Director	Fabien Baron
Art Director	Joel Berg
Photographer	Patrick Demarchelier
Publisher	The Hearst Corporation
Category	Design/Single Page or Spread
Date	September 1992

remember a time when genders were bent, rules broken, inhibitions shed, and all the best girls were pretty wild?

The Buffalo Girl tangles with Sergeant Pepper. This page: Velvet coat, about $2995, white organza blouse, about $655, and black rayon shorts, about $195. All from Ozbek. Hat, Phillip Treacy; necklace, Alan McDonald, both for Ozbek.

Publication Entertainment Weekly
Award Silver
Design Director Michael Grossman
Art Director Arlene Lappen
Designer Gregory Mastrianni
Illustrators Mark Tucker, Gina Binkley
Publisher Entertainment Weekly, Inc.
Category Illustration/Single Page or Spread
Date April 24, 1992

Harlem Nocturnes

Anchored in the energies of New York between the wars, Toni Morrison's sixth novel is a
soaring improvisation that ranks with the best American fiction. BY THOMAS M. DISCH

SONGS IN PRAISE of New York City were once a staple of Tin Pan Alley, but not since Kander and Ebb's 1977 hit, "New York, New York," has there been a great new unofficial anthem. Novelists also used to vie for the honor of celebrating the Great American Urban Magnet, though with novelists it was usually a love-hate relationship until sometime around 1964, with *Last Exit to Brooklyn*, when hate began to gain a monopoly. But here at last is Toni Morrison's *JAZZ (Knopf, $21)*, a novel that is one long, hyperlyrical love song to the state of mind she calls "the City."

Morrison's particular beat is Harlem, circa 1926, which she pictures as an almost utopian haven for "the wave of black people running from [the] want and violence" of the hinterlands. There,

even if the room they rented was smaller than the heifer's stall and darker than a morning privy, they stayed to look at their number, hear themselves in an audience, feel themselves moving down the street among hundreds of others who moved the way they did, and who, when they spoke, regardless of the accent, treated language like the same intricate, malleable toy designed for their play." Even more than in her Pulitzer Prize–winning 1987 novel, *Beloved*, Morrison plays with language with the flair of a virtuoso. *Jazz* isn't called *Jazz* because it's about jazz musicians, but because its prose is the verbal equivalent—long, looping improvisations full of recognizable blues melodies on the subjects of love, death, jealous rage, the serenity of reconciliation—that never go quite where you think they're going. The story flows

along so freely that no one, not even the author herself, can second-guess how it will end. The springboard for Morrison's music is the murder by a 50-year-old cosmetics salesman, Joe Trace, of his teenage mistress, Dorcas. His wife, Violet, attacks the girl's corpse at her funeral and afterwards is obsessed with finding out everything she can about her. This much we learn in the first pages, and all that follows is an investigation of the roots of Joe's, Violet's, and Dorcas' behavior, an inquiry that takes Morrison back to the antebellum South.

To my ear the passages back in Vesper County lack the textured richness of Morrison's portraits of life in jazz-era Harlem—or the fierceness of her treatment of the slave states in *Beloved*. But these chapters make up only a short parenthesis toward the end of what is otherwise a wholly satisfying novel. One of its major satisfactions is its chess-masterly cleverness in playing the literary game called Point of View, a game that in *Jazz* is not at all a trivial pursuit. Morrison has a keen, analytical awareness of where a "voice" is coming from, and the significance that the sourcing of a writer's voice can have. Witness her simultaneously published essay *Playing in the Dark: Whiteness and the Literary Imagination* (Harvard University Press), a study of how tricky even the simplest-seeming writer can be; she's that tricky herself.

So many novelists, both black and white, begin strong and then somehow slack off. Toni Morrison began strong and has moved from strength to strength until she has reached the distinction of being beyond comparison. Someday, I'm sure, her name will appear on the spine of a Library of American edition, alongside the works of Richard Wright and Flannery O'Connor. Meanwhile we can enjoy her latest masterpiece in its first edition. **A**

EXCERPT

The Shape of Things to Come

I'M CRAZY about this City.

Daylight slants like a razor cutting the buildings in half. In the top half I see looking faces and it's not easy to tell which are people, which the work of stonemasons. Below is shadow where any blue thing takes place: clarinets and lovemaking, fists and the voices of sorrowful women. A city like this one makes me dream tall and feel in on things. Hep. It's the bright steel rocking above the shade below that does it. When I look over strips of green grass lining the river, at church steeples and into the cream-and-copper halls of apartment buildings, I'm strong. Alone, yes, but top-notch and indestructible—like the City in 1926 when all the wars are over and there will never be another one. The people down there in the shadow are happy about that. At last, at last, everything's ahead. The smart ones say so and people listening to them and reading what they write down agree: Here comes the new. Look out. There goes the sad stuff. The bad stuff. The things-nobody-could-help stuff. The way everybody was then and there. Forget that. History is over, you all, and everything's ahead at last. In halls and offices people are sitting around thinking future thoughts about projects and bridges and fast-clicking trains underneath.

58 APRIL 24, 1992 · PHOTO ILLUSTRATION BY MARK TUCKER/GINA BINKLEY · ENTERTAINMENT WEEKLY 59

Publication Harper's Bazaar
Award Silver
Creative Director Fabien Baron
Art Director Joel Berg
Photographer Mario Testino
Publisher The Hearst Corporation
Category Design/Single Page or Spread
Date December 1992

Not everyone migrates south
for the winter. The snow bunny
hits the slopes in flashes of
silver and puffs of marabou
that zip right down to sexy.

Publication Ray Gun
Award Silver
Design Director David Carson
Designer David Carson
Photographer John Severson
Publisher Ray Gun
Studio David Carson Design
Category Design/Single Page or Spread
Date November 1992

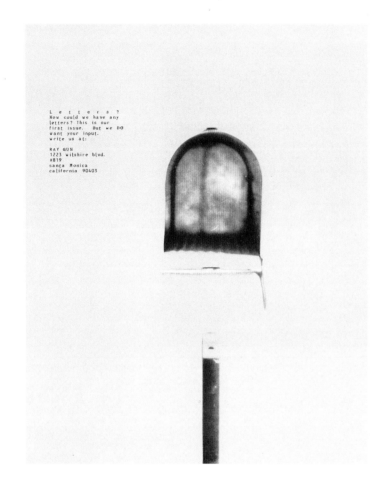

Publication Rolling Stone
Award Silver
Art Director Fred Woodward
Designer Fred Woodward
Photographer Herb Ritts
Photo Editor Laurie Kratochvil
Publisher Straight Arrow Publishers, Inc.
Category Design/Single Page or Spread
Date September 3, 1992

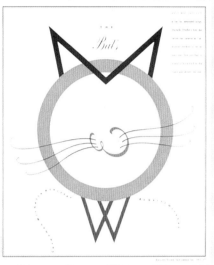

Publication Digital News
Award Silver
Art Director Mark Koudys
Designer Mark Koudys
Photographer Ron Baxter Smith
Studio Atlanta Art & Design
Client Digital Equipment of Canada
Category Design/Single Page or Spread
Date November 1992

Publication American Heritage
Award Merit
Art Director Peter Morance
Designer Peter Morance
Photo Editor Catherine Calhoun
Publisher American Heritage
Category Design/Single Page or Spread
Date May/June 1992

Publication Aspen Aces and Eights
Award Merit
Design Director Holly Jaffe
Art Director Holly Jaffe
Designer Nicholas DeVore III
Photo Editor Ernest Vogliano
Publisher Aspen Aces and Eights, Inc.
Category Design/Single Page or Spread
Date December 1992

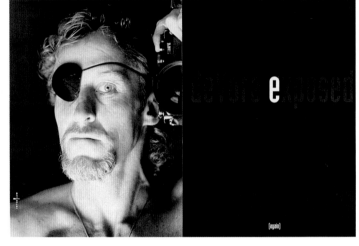

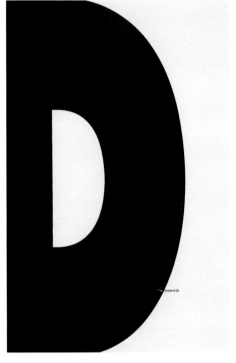

Publication Country America
Award Merit
Design Director Jerry J. Rank
Art Director Jerry J. Rank
Designer Jerry J. Rank
Photographer Robin Hood
Photo Editor Jerry J. Rank
Publisher Meredith Corporation
Studio Jerry J. Rank
Category Design/Single Page or Spread
Date September 1992

Publication Creem
Award Merit
Art Director Scott Menchin
Designers Scott Menchin, Eric Rochow
Illustrator Stevenson
Publisher Creem
Category Design/Single Page or Spread
Date March 1992

Publication	Details
Award	Merit
Design Director	B.W. Honeycutt
Art Director	B.W. Honeycutt
Designer	Markus Kiersztan
Photographer	Enrique Badulescu
Photo Editor	Greg Pond
Publisher	Condé Nast Publishing Co., Inc.
Category	Design/Single Page or Spread
Date	April 1992

Publication	Details
Award	Merit
Design Director	B.W. Honeycutt
Art Director	B.W. Honeycutt
Designer	Markus Kiersztan
Photographer	Dan Winters
Photo Editor	Greg Pond
Publisher	Condé Nast Publishing Co., Inc.
Category	Design/Single Page or Spread
Date	December 1992

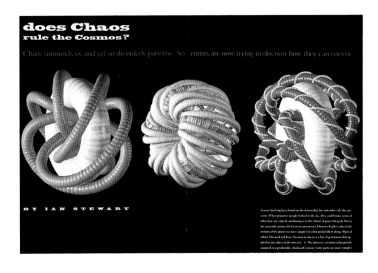

Publication	Discover
Award	Merit
Art Directors	David Armario, James Lambertus
Designer	James Lambertus
Photographer	Roger Ressmeyer
Photo Editor	John Barker
Publisher	Disney Magazine Publishing
Category	Design/Single Page or Spread
Date	November 1992

Publication	Discover
Award	Merit
Design Director	David Armario
Art Directors	David Armario, James Lambertus
Designer	James Lambertus
Photo Editor	John Barker
Publisher	Disney Magazine Publishing
Category	Design/Single Page or Spread
Date	November 1992

Publication	Discover
Award	Merit
Design Director	David Armario
Art Directors	David Armario, James Lambertus
Designers	James Lambertus, David Armario
Photographer	Geof Kern
Photo Editor	John Baker
Publisher	Disney Magazine Publishing
Category	Design/Single Page or Spread
Date	September 1992

Publication	Entertainment Weekly
Award	Merit
Design Director	Michael Grossman
Art Director	Mark Michaelson
Photographer	Jeffery Newbury
Photo Editors	Mary Dunn, Mark Jacobson
Publisher	Entertainment Weekly, Inc.
Category	Design/Single Page or Spread
Date	March 6, 1992

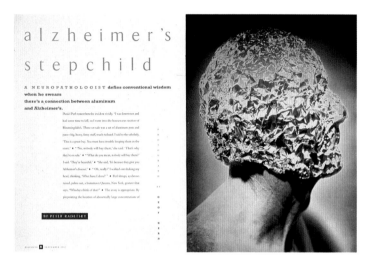

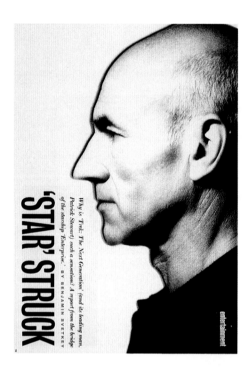

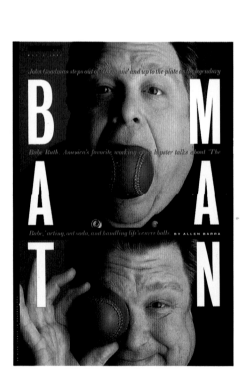

Publication	Entertainment Weekly
Award	Merit
Design Director	Michael Grossman
Art Director	Mark Michaelson
Designer	Miriam Campiz
Photographer	Darryl Estrine
Photo Editors	Mary Dunn, Doris Brautigan
Publisher	Entertainment Weekly, Inc.
Category	Design/Single Page or Spread
Date	May 1, 1992

Publication	Entertainment Weekly
Award	Merit
Design Director	Michael Grossman
Art Director	Mark Michaelson
Designer	Miriam Campiz
Photographer	Darryl Estrine
Photo Editors	Mary Dunn, Doris Brautigan
Publisher	Entertainment Weekly, Inc.
Category	Design/Single Page or Spread
Date	May 1, 1992

Publication Entertainment Weekly
Award Merit
Design Director Michael Grossman
Art Director Mark Michaelson
Illustrator Michael Delsol
Photographer Michael Delsol
Photo Editor Mary Dunn
Publisher Entertainment Weekly, Inc.
Category Design/Single Page or Spread
Date September 25, 1992

Publication Entertainment Weekly
Award Merit
Design Director Michael Grossman
Art Director Mark Michaelson
Photographer Mark Hanaver
Photo Editors Mary Dunn, Doris Brautigan
Publisher Entertainment Weekly, Inc.
Category Design/Single Page or Spread
Date June 19, 1992

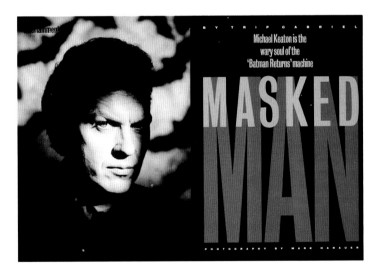

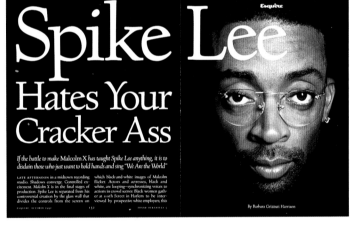

Publication Entertainment Weekly
Award Merit
Design Director Michael Grossman
Art Director Mark Michaelson
Designer Miriam Campiz
Photographer Mark Hanaver
Photo Editor Mary Dunn, Doris Brautigan
Publisher Entertainment Weekly, Inc.
Category Design/Single Page or Spread
Date June 19, 1992

Publication Esquire
Award Merit
Design Director Rhonda Rubinstein
Art Director Rhonda Rubinstein
Photographer Frank W. Ockenfels 3
Photo Editor Betsy Horan
Publisher The Hearst Corporation
Category Design/Single Page or Spread
Date October 1992

Publication	Garbage
Award	Merit
Design Director	Patrick Mitchell
Designer	Patrick Mitchell
Photographer	Deborah Samuel
Publisher	Dovetale Publishers
Category	Design/Single Page or Spread
Date	May/June 1992

Publication	Four Seasons Magazine
Award	Merit
Art Director	Mark Koudys
Designers	Mark Koudys, Joyce Nesnadny
Photographers	John Lloyd, Nancy Saxberg
Publisher	Atlanta Art and Design
Studio	Atlanta Art and Design
Client	Four Seasons Hotels and Resorts
Category	Design/Single Page or Spread
Date	August 1992

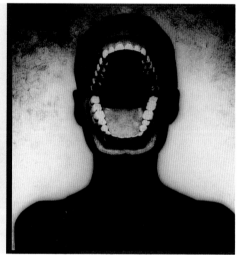

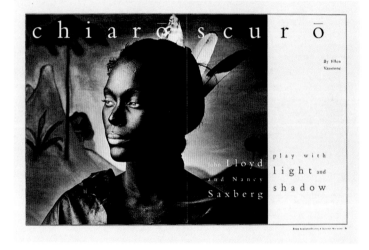

Publication	Harper's Bazaar
Award	Merit
Creative Director	Fabien Baron
Art Director	Joel Berg
Designer	Johan Svensson
Photographer	Paolo Roversi
Publisher	The Hearst Corporation
Category	Design/Single Page or Spread
Date	November 1992

Publication	Harper's Bazaar
Award	Merit
Creative Director	Fabien Baron
Art Director	Joel Berg
Photographer	Patrik Andersson
Publisher	The Hearst Corporation
Category	Design/Single Page or Spread
Date	November 1992

With "Bram Stoker's Dracula," director Francis Ford Coppola creates a vampire legend for our time. By Laurie Winer

deathbecomeshim

madame X

Publication	Harper's Bazaar
Award	Merit
Creative Director	Fabien Baron
Art Director	Joel Berg
Designer	Johan Svensson
Photographer	Ron Gallela
Publisher	The Hearst Corporation
Category	Design/Single Page or Spread
Date	October 1992

gathering MOSS

Understanding the conundrums designed by L.A.'s unpredictable architect Eric Owen Moss isn't always easy—but what works by an enfant terrible are?
By Joseph Giovannini

Publication	Harper's Bazaar
Award	Merit
Creative Director	Fabien Baron
Design Director	Fabien Baron
Art Director	Joel Berg
Photographer	Michel Arnaud
Publisher	The Hearst Corporation
Category	Design/Single Page or Spread
Date	September 1992

Publication Harper's Bazaar
Award Merit
Creative Director Fabien Baron
Art Director Joel Berg
Photographer Patrick Demarchelier
Publisher The Hearst Corporation
Category Design/Single Page or Spread
Date September 1992

Publication LA Style
Award Merit
Design Director Lloyd Ziff
Art Director Margot Frankel
Designer Steven Hankinson
Photographer Matthew Rolston
Photo Editor Bill Swan
Publisher American Express Publishing
Category Design/Single Page or Spread
Date December 1992

Publication Harper's Bazaar
Award Merit
Creative Director Fabien Baron
Art Director Joel Berg
Publisher The Hearst Corporation
Category Design/Single Page or Spread
Date December 1992

Publication	LA Style
Award	Merit
Design Director	Lloyd Ziff
Designer	Kim Cruser
Photographer	Hervé Grison
Photo Editor	Bill Swan
Publisher	American Express Publishing
Category	Design/Single Page or Spread
Date	June 1992

Publication	LA Style
Award	Merit
Design Director	Lloyd Ziff
Art Director	Margot Frankel
Designer	Kim Cruser
Photographer	Andrew Eccles
Photo Editor	Bill Swan
Publisher	American Express Publishing
Category	Design/Single Page or Spread
Date	November 1992

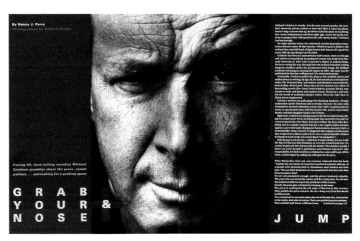

Publication	Mohawk Paper Promotion
Award	Merit
Design Director	Michael Bierut
Art Director	Michael Bierut
Designers	Michael Bierut, Lisa Cerveny
Studio	Pentagram Design, NYC
Client	Mohawk Paper Mills
Category	Design/Single Page or Spread
Date	Fall 1992

Publication Harper's Bazaar
Award Merit
Creative Director Fabien Baron
Art Director Joel Berg
Designer Johan Svensson
Illustrators Ellsworth Kelly, Agnes Martin
Publisher The Hearst Corporation
Category Design/Single Page or Spread
Date October 1992

Publication Harper's Bazaar
Award Merit
Creative Director Fabien Baron
Art Director Joel Berg
Photographer Frederick Lieberath
Publisher The Hearst Corporation
Category Design/Single Page or Spread
Date December 1992

PURE
Abstraction

Two upcoming museum shows celebrate the
work of Agnes Martin and Ellsworth Kelly, artists
who have kept the faith. By Lisa Liebmann

Contraceptive Choice
Depo-Provera sounds like the
perfect form of birth control:
injectable, affordable, effective,
and relatively safe. So why has it
raised more questions on the
contraceptive options available to
women than it has answered?
Ellen Hopkins reports.

Redefining the boundaries of fashion:
the season's important, impeccable menswear looks,
and the brilliant contradiction of women who
claim tailoring as their own, not in emulation,
but for its straightforward manner, its
ability to take forms as studied, or abandoned,
as the impulses of the wearer.

No Man's Land

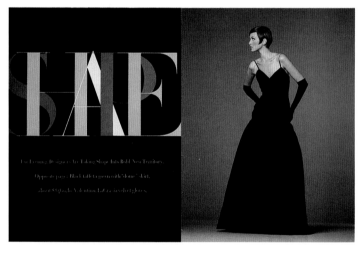

Publication Harper's Bazaar
Award Merit
Creative Director Fabien Baron
Art Director Joel Berg
Photographer Peter Lindbergh
Publisher The Hearst Corporation
Category Design/Single Page or Spread
Date September 1992

Publication Harper's Bazaar
Award Merit
Creative Director Fabien Baron
Art Director Joel Berg
Designer Johan Svensson
Photographer Mario Testino
Publisher The Hearst Corporation
Category Design/Single Page or Spread
Date November 1992

Publication	Harper's Bazaar
Award	Merit
Creative Director	Fabien Baron
Art Director	Joel Berg
Designer	Johan Svensson
Photographer	Michel Arnaud
Publisher	The Hearst Corporation
Category	Design/Single Page or Spread
Date	December 1992

Publication	Harper's Bazaar
Award	Merit
Creative Director	Fabien Baron
Design Director	Fabien Baron
Art Director	Joel Berg
Photographer	Stephen Anderson
Publisher	The Hearst Corporation
Category	Design/Single Page or Spread
Date	October 1992

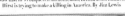

Publication	Harper's Bazaar
Award	Merit
Creative Director	Fabien Baron
Art Director	Joel Berg
Publisher	The Hearst Corporation
Category	Design/Single Page or Spread
Date	November 1992

Publication	Harper's Bazaar
Award	Merit
Creative Director	Fabien Baron
Art Director	Joel Berg
Publisher	The Hearst Corporation
Category	Design/Single Page or Spread
Date	January 1992

Publication Health
Award Merit
Art Director Jane Palecek
Designer Dorothy Marschall
Photographer Pete McArthur
Publisher Health
Category Design/Single Page or Spread
Date January 1992

Publication Hemispheres
Award Merit
Design Director Kit Hinrichs
Art Directors Kit Hinrichs, Jaimey Easler
Designer Jackie Foshaug
Photographer Terry Heffernan
Publisher Pace Communications
Studio Pentagram Design
Client United Airlines
Category Design/Single Page or Spread
Date October 1992

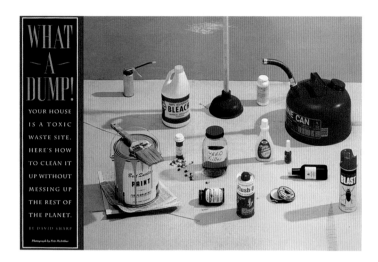

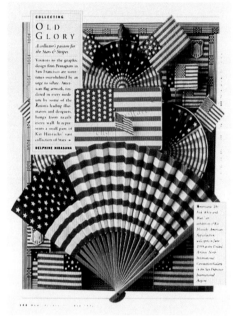

Publication Life
Award Merit
Design Director Tom Bentkowski
Art Director Tom Bentkowski
Designer Marty Golon
Photographers Everett Collection, Harry Benson
Publisher Time Inc. Magazine Company
Category Design/Single Page or Spread
Date May 1992

Publication Men's Journal
Award Merit
Art Director Matthew Drace
Designer Matthew Drace
Photographer Len Irish
Publisher Straight Arrow Publishers
Category Design/Single Page or Spread
Date November/December 1992

Publication Men's Journal
Award Merit
Art Director Matthew Drace
Designers Matthew Drace, Giovanni Russo
Illustrator Roxanna Villa
Photographer George Holz
Publisher Straight Arrow Publishers
Category Design/Single Page or Spread

Publication Metropolis
Award Merit
Art Directors Carl Lehmann-Haupt, Nancy Cohen
Designers Carl Lehmann-Haupt, Nancy Cohen
Publisher Bellerophon Publications, Inc.
Category Design/Single Page or Spread
Date January/Feburary 1992

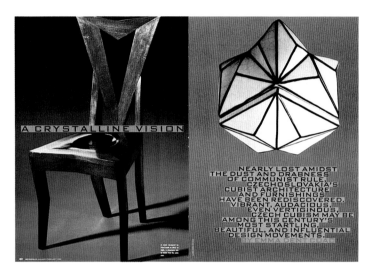

Publication Mother Jones
Award Merit
Art Director Marsha Sessa
Designer Marsha Sessa
Photographer Robert McKeown
Publisher Foundation for National Progress
Category Design/Single Page or Spread
Date May/June 1992

Publication New York
Award Merit
Design Director Robert Best
Designers Robert Best, Syndi Becker, Kathryn DelVecchio
Photographer William Wegman
Publisher K-III Magazines
Category Design/Single Page or Spread
Date March 1992

Publication PC World
Award Merit
Design Director Mitch Shostak
Art Director Greg Silva
Designer Greg Silva
Illustrator Gordon Studer
Publisher PCW Communications, Inc.
Category Design/Single Page or Spread
Date February 1992

Publication Ray Gun
Award Merit
Design Director David Carson
Illustrator Matt Mahurin
Photographer Matt Mahurin
Publisher Ray Gun
Studio David Carson Design
Category Design/Single Page or Spread
Date December 1992

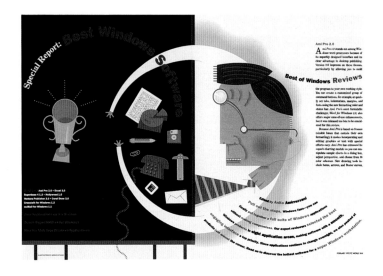

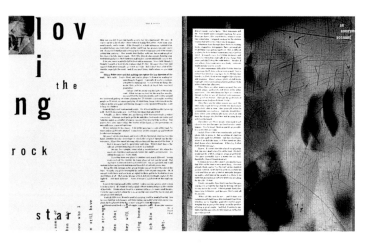

Publication Ray Gun
Award Merit
Design Director David Carson
Art Director David Carson
Photographer Glen Erler
Publisher Ray Gun
Studio David Carson Design
Category Design/Single Page or Spread
Date December 1992

Publication Ray Gun
Award Merit
Design Director David Carson
Art Director David Carson
Photographer Diana Klien
Publisher Ray Gun
Studio David Carson Design
Category Design/Single Page or Spread
Date November 1992

Publication Rolling Stone
Award Merit
Art Director Fred Woodward
Designer Fred Woodward
Photographer Albert Watson
Photo Editor Laurie Kratochvil
Publisher Straight Arrow Publishers, Inc.
Category Design/Single Page or Spread
Date July 9, 1992

Publication Rolling Stone
Award Merit
Art Director Fred Woodward
Designer Fred Woodward
Photographer Albert Watson
Photo Editor Laurie Kratochvil
Publisher Straight Arrow Publishers, Inc.
Category Design/Single Page or Spread
Date February 6, 1992

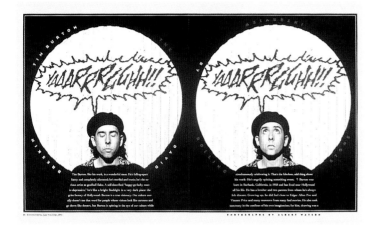

Publication Rolling Stone
Award Merit
Art Director Fred Woodward
Designer Gail Anderson
Photographer Albert Watson
Photo Editor Laurie Kratochvil
Publisher Straight Arrow Publishers, Inc.
Category Design/Single Page or Spread
Date November 26, 1992

Publication Rolling Stone
Award Merit
Art Director Fred Woodward
Designer Debra Bishop
Photographer Albert Watson
Photo Editor Laurie Kratochvil
Publisher Straight Arrow Publishers, Inc.
Category Design/Single Page or Spread
Date March 5, 1992

Publication Rolling Stone
Award Merit
Art Director Fred Woodward
Designer Debra Bishop
Photographer Mark Seliger
Photo Editor Laurie Kratochvil
Publisher Straight Arrow Publishers, Inc.
Category Design/Single Page or Spread
Date July 25, 1992

Publication Rolling Stone
Award Merit
Art Director Fred Woodward
Designer Debra Bishop
Photographer Mark Seliger
Photo Editor Laurie Kratochvil
Publisher Straight Arrow Publishers, Inc.
Category Design/Single Page or Spread
Date August 20, 1992

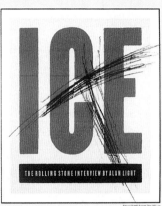

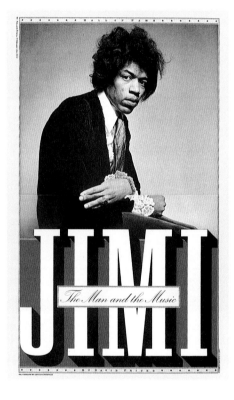

Publication Rolling Stone
Award Merit
Art Director Fred Woodward
Designer Catherine Gilmore-Barnes
Photographer Frank W. Ockenfels 3
Photo Editor Laurie Kratochvil
Publisher Straight Arrow Publishers, Inc.
Category Design/Single Page or Spread
Date March 19, 1992

Publication Rolling Stone
Award Merit
Art Director Fred Woodward
Designer Catherine Gilmore-Barnes
Photographer Gered Mankowitz
Photo Editor Laurie Kratochvil
Publisher Straight Arrow Publishers, Inc.
Category Design/Single Page or Spread
Date February 6, 1992

Publication	Rolling Stone
Award	Merit
Art Director	Fred Woodward
Designer	Fred Woodward
Illustrator	Philip Burke
Publisher	Straight Arrow Publishers, Inc.
Category	Design/Single Page or Spread
Date	October 1, 1992

Publication	Rolling Stone
Award	Merit
Art Director	Fred Woodward
Designer	Angela Skouras
Photographer	Albert Watson
Photo Editor	Laurie Kratochvil
Publisher	Straight Arrow Publishers, Inc.
Category	Design/Single Page or Spread
Date	October 29, 1992

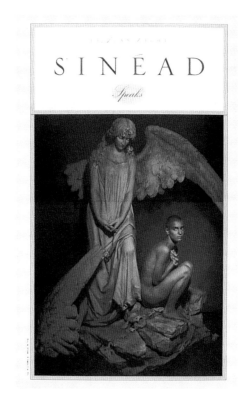

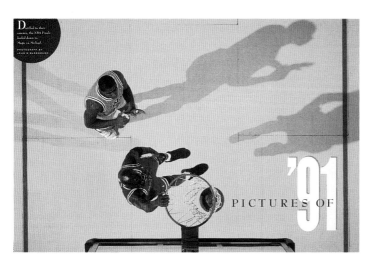

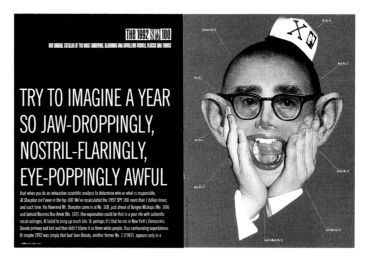

Publication	Sports Illustrated
Award	Merit
Design Director	Steven Hoffman
Designer	Ed Truscio
Photographer	John W. McDonough
Photo Editor	Karen Mullarkey
Publisher	Time Inc. Magazine Company
Category	Design/Single Page or Spread
Date	December 1991/January 1992

Publication	SPY
Award	Merit
Art Director	Christiaan Kuypers
Designers	Christiaan Kuypers, Daniel Carter
Illustrators	Christiaan Kuypers, Ron Meckler
Publisher	Spy Corporation
Category	Design/Single Page or Spread
Date	December 1992/January 1993 Double Issue

Publication Steamboat
Award Merit
Creative Director Laurie Feiterouf
Photographers Larry Pierce, Jim Steinberg
Studio Steamboat Communications Group, Inc.
Category Design/Single Page or Spread
Date Winter 1993

Publication Traces
Award Merit
Design Director R. Lloyd Brooks
Designer R. Lloyd Brooks
Photographer Wilbur Montgomery
Publisher Indiana Historical Society
Studio Dean Johnson Design
Client Kent Calder
Category Design/Single Page or Spread
Date Fall 1992

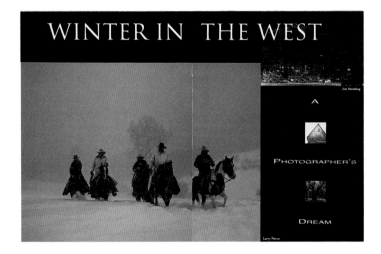

Publication Travel Holiday
Award Merit
Art Director Lou Di Lorenzo
Designer Lou Di Lorenzo
Photographer Dennis Marsico
Photo Editor Bill Black
Publisher Readers Digest Publications
Studio Travel Holiday
Category Design/Single Page or Spread
Date November 1992

Publication Vibe
Award Merit
Design Director Gary Koepke
Art Director Gary Koepke
Designer Diddo Ramm
Photographer Albert Watson
Studio Koepke Design Group
Category Design/Single Page or Spread
Date Preview

Publication Adweek
Award Merit
Art Director Carole Erger-Fass
Designer Blake Taylor
Photographer Frank Veronsky
Publisher Adweek, L.P.
Category Design/Single Page or Spread
Date November 2, 1992

Publication Brandweek
Award Merit
Art Director Carole Erger-Fass
Photographer Chip Simons
Photo Editor Carmin Romanelli
Publisher Adweek, L.P.
Category Design/Single Page or Spread
Date October 19, 1992

Publication Adweek
Award Merit
Art Director Carole Erger-Fass
Designer Blake Taylor
Photographer Alain Keler / Matrix
Photo Editor Sabine Meyer
Publisher Adweek, L.P.
Category Design/Single Page or Spread
Date November 23, 1992

Publication Adweek
Award Merit
Art Director Carole Erger-Fass
Designers Keith Christensen, Alan Ball
Photographer FPG International
Photo Editor Carmin Romanelli
Publisher Adweek, L.P.
Category Design/Single Page or Spread
Date June 22, 1992

Publication CIO
Award Merit
Design Director Mary Marshall
Art Director Mary Marshall
Designer Mary Marshall
Photographer Jack Van Antwerp
Publisher CIO Publishing
Category Design/Single Page or Spread
Date June 1, 1992

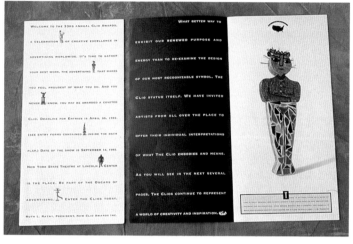

Publication Clio Brochure
Award Merit
Art Director John Muller
Designers John Muller, James Dettner
Photographer Mike Regnier
Studio Muller + Company
Category Design/Single Page or Spread

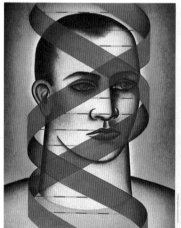

Publication Diabetes Forecast
Award Merit
Art Director Tom Suzuki
Designer Timothy Cook
Illustrator Sandra Dionisi
Studio Tom Suzuki, Inc.
Client American Diabetes Association
Category Design/Single Page or Spread
Date May 1992

Publication	Diabetes Forecast
Award	Merit
Art Director	Tom Suzuki
Designer	Timothy Cook
Illustrator	Leslie Cober
Studio	Tom Suzuki, Inc.
Client	American Diabetes Association
Category	Design/Single Page or Spread
Date	November 1992

Publication	Forbes FYI
Award	Merit
Art Director	Alexander Isley
Designer	Lynette Cortez
Illustrator	Ross MacDonald
Publisher	Forbes, Inc.
Studio	Alexander Isley Design
Category	Design/Single Page or Spread
Date	September 1992

THANKSGIVING IN BLUEGRASS COUNTRY

America's Bluegrass state welcomes you at its Thanksgiving Day feast. When Kentucky is mentioned anywhere in the United States—or the world—people think of the Kentucky Derby, bourbon whiskey, and bluegrass music. But there's a lot more to Kentucky than tips, sips, and fast licks. First, and always, there is the land: the rolling green hills, the hollows, the fertile fields. There are also historic waterways: the Ohio, which forms Kentucky's northern border, the Cumberland, and the Kentucky Rivers. Then there are the people, who this year are celebrating.

by Debbie Fillman

LEAR ON SKIS

BY ALISTAIR HORNE

ike Lear, I have three daughters. When it comes to skiing, that brutal activity which brings out both the best and the worst of human instincts, I never dared to speculate on which would prove to be nice Cordelia—or the nasty ones with names like a social disease and a former President. But experience on the slopes, an estimated sum-total of 65 years of togetherness and occasional disputes, suggests possibly a combination of both.

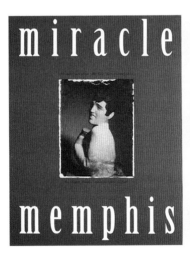

Publication	Ego
Award	Merit
Art Director	Ted Fabella
Designer	Ted Fabella
Photographer	Peter Fownes
Studio	Ted Fabella
Client	Creative Club of Atlanta
Category	Design/Single Page or Spread
Date	March 1992

Publication	Ego
Award	Merit
Art Director	Ted Fabella
Designer	Ted Fabella
Illustrator	Bill Mayer
Studio	Ted Fabella
Client	Creative Club of Atlanta
Category	Design/Single Page or Spread
Date	March 1992

Publication	Forbes FYI
Award	Merit
Art Director	Alexander Isley
Designer	Lynette Cortez
Illustrator	Paul Bachem
Publisher	Forbes, Inc.
Studio	Alexander Isley Design
Category	Design/Single Page or Spread
Date	November 1992

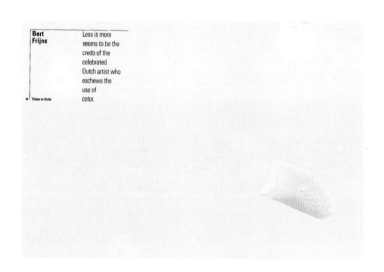

Publication	Graphis
Award	Merit
Design Director	B. Martin Pedersen
Art Directors	Randell Pearson, B. Martin Pedersen
Designer	B. Martin Pedersen
Publisher	Graphis US, Inc.
Category	Design/Single Page or Spread
Date	November/December 1992

Publication	Glass
Award	Merit
Design Director	Michael Bierut
Designer	Michael Bierut
Photographer	V.E. Meuwenhuijs
Studio	Pentagram Design
Client	New York Experimental Glass Workshop
Category	Design/Single Page or Spread
Date	Winter 1992

Publication Graphis
Award Merit
Design Director B. Martin Pedersen
Art Director Randell Pearson
Designer B. Martin Pedersen
Photographer Arnold Neuman
Publisher Graphis US, Inc.
Category Design/Single Page or Spread
Date January/February 1992

Publication Hippocrates
Award Merit
Art Director Jane Palecek
Designer Alicia Keshishian
Illustrator Janet Woolley
Publisher Hippocrates
Category Design/Single Page or Spread
Date October 1992

Publication Graphis
Award Merit
Design Director B. Martin Pedersen
Art Directors B. Martin Pedersen, Randell Pearson
Designer B. Martin Pedersen
Photographer Poul Ilb Henriksen
Publisher Graphis US, Inc.
Category Design/Single Page or Spread
Date May/June 1992

Publication U&lc
Award Merit
Art Director Seymour Chwast
Designer Greg Simpson
Publisher International Typeface Corporation
Studio Pushpin Group Inc.
Category Design/Single Page or Spread
Date Fall 1992

Publication Scholastic Scope
Award Merit
Design Director Will Kefauver
Art Directors Joy Toltzis Makon, John Olenyik
Photographer Jim Porto
Publisher Scholastic. Inc.
Category Design/Single Page or Spread
Date February 21, 1992

Publication U&lc
Award Merit
Art Director Seymour Chwast
Designer Greg Simpson
Publisher International Typeface Corporation
Studio Pushpin Group Inc.
Category Design/Single Page or Spread
Date Fall 1992

Publication U&lc
Award Merit
Design Directors Milton Glaser, Walter Bernard
Designer Milton Glaser
Illustrator Mirko Ilic
Studio WBMG, Inc.
Category Design/Single Page or Spread
Date Spring 1992

Publication	Varbusiness
Award	Merit
Design Director	Joe McNeill
Art Directors	David Loewy, Renee Bundi, Andrea Pinto
Designer	David Loewy
Publisher	CMP Publications
Category	Design/Single Page or Spread
Date	April 1992

Publication	Varbusiness
Award	Merit
Design Director	Joe McNeill
Art Directors	David Loewy, Renee Bundi, Andrea Pinto
Designer	Renee Bundi
Illustrator	Elwood Smith
Publisher	CMP Publications
Category	Design/Single Page or Spread
Date	April 1992

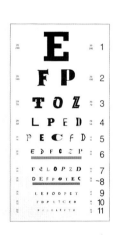

Publication	Varbusiness
Award	Merit
Design Director	Joe McNeill
Art Directors	David Loewy, Renee Bundi, Andrea Pinto
Designer	David Loewy
Publisher	CMP Publications
Category	Design/Single Page or Spread
Date	November 1992

Publication	Wordperfect for Windows
Award	Merit
Art Director	Ron Stucki
Designer	Ron Stucki
Illustrator	Gary Whitehead
Publisher	Wordperfect Publishing
Category	Design/Single Page or Spread
Date	April 2, 1992

Publication Wordperfect for Windows
Award Merit
Art Director Ron Stucki
Designer Ron Stucki
Illustrator Paula Scher
Publisher Wordperfect Publishing
Category Design/Single Page or Spread
Date April 1992

Publication The Washington Lawyer
Award Merit
Art Director Glenn Pierce
Designer Glenn Pierce
Illustrator Scott Roberts
Publisher The Magazine Group
Category Design/Single Page or Spread
Date January/February 1992

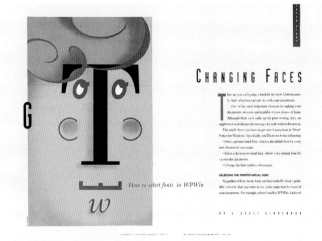

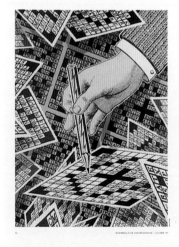

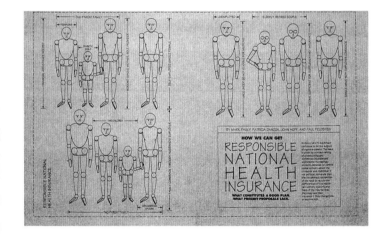

Publication Wordperfect for Windows
Award Merit
Art Director Ron Stucki
Designer Ron Stucki
Illustrator John Craig
Publisher Wordperfect Publishing
Category Design/Single Page or Spread
Date October 1992

Publication The American Enterprise
Award Merit
Design Director Paula Duggan
Art Directors Paula Duggan, Liz Clark
Designer Liz Clark
Illustrator Liz Clark
Category Design/Single Page or Spread
Date July/August 1992

Publication Discovery
Award Merit
Design Director Andrea Koura
Art Director Percy Chung
Designer Percy Chung
Photographers R. Ian Lloyd, Percy Chung
Photo Editor Cathy Whitfield
Publisher Empasis Co. Ltd., Hong Kong
Client Cathay Pacific Airways
Category Design/Single Page or Spread
Date August 1992

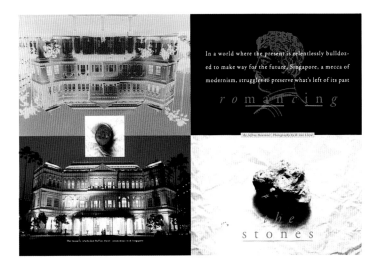

Publication Discovery
Award Merit
Design Director Andrea Koura
Art Director Andrea Koura
Designer Andrea Koura
Photographer Martin Richardson
Photo Editor Cathy Whitfield
Publisher Empasis Co. Ltd., Hong Kong
Client Cathay Pacific Airways
Category Design/Single Page or Spread
Date December 1992

Publication Discovery
Award Merit
Design Director Percy Chung
Art Director Percy Chung
Designer Percy Chung
Illustrator Ka-Sing Lee
Photo Editor Cathy Whitfield
Publisher Empasis (H.K.) Co. Ltd.
Client Cathay Pacific Airways
Category Design/Single Page or Spread
Date November 1992

Publication	Digital News
Award	Merit
Design Director	Mark Koudys
Designer	Mark Koudys
Photographer	Ron Baker Smith
Studio	Atlanta Art and Design
Client	Digital Equipment of Canada
Category	Design/Single Page or Spread
Date	August 1992

Publication	Digital News
Award	Merit
Design Director	Mark Koudys
Designer	Mark Koudys
Photographer	Ron Baker Smith
Studio	Atlanta Art and Design
Client	Digital Equipment of Canada
Category	Design/Single Page or Spread
Date	August 1992

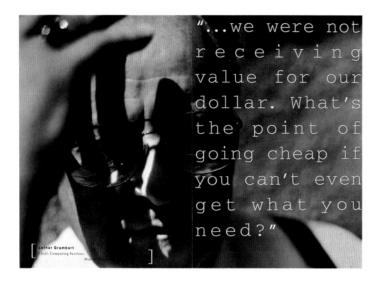

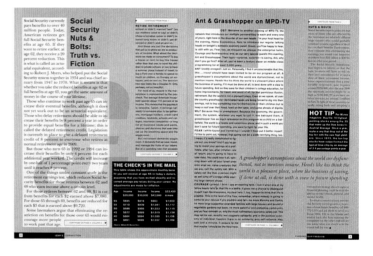

Publication	Lear's "Connection" Newsletter
Award	Merit
Design Director	Bruce Ramsay
Art Director	Paula Kelly
Designer	Paula Kelly
Publisher	Lear's Publishing
Category	Design/Single Page or Spread
Date	Vol. 1, No. 4 1992

Publication	Lear's "Connection" Newsletter
Award	Merit
Design Director	Bruce Ramsay
Art Director	Paula Kelly
Designer	Paula Kelly
Photographer	Paula Kelly
Publisher	Lear's Publishing
Category	Design/Single Page or Spread
Date	Vol. 1, No. 2 1992

Publication Salon Styling with Vidal Sassoon
Award Merit
Design Director David Orr
Art Director David Orr
Designer David Orr
Photographers Wolfgang Ludes, Roger Cabello
Photo Editor Dianne Fishman
Publisher Fishman Creative Associates
Studio Doubling Communication
Client Proctor and Gamble
Category Design/Single Page or Spread
Date November 1992

Publication Stanford Magazine
Award Merit
Art Director Paul Carstensen
Designer Paul Carstensen
Illustrator Amy Guip
Publisher Stanford Alumni Association
Category Design/Single Page or Spread
Date December 1992

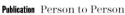

Publication Person to Person
Award Merit
Design Director Robert Petrick
Art Director Robert Petrick
Designers Robert Petrick, Laura Ress
Photo Editor Laura Ress
Studio Petrick Design
Category Design/Single Page or Spread
Date November 1992

Publication Show Offs
Award Merit
Art Directors Jan Ellis, Laurie Ellis
Designers Jan Ellis, Laurie Ellis
Photographer Mark Tucker
Studio Ellis Design
Client Athens Paper
Category Design/Single Page or Spread
Date July 1992

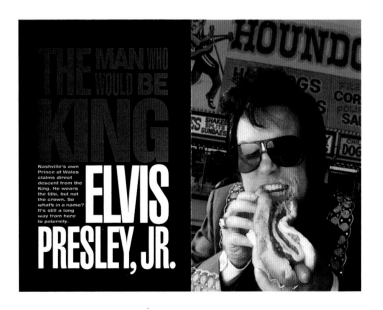

Publication Show Offs
Award Merit
Art Directors Jan Ellis, Laurie Ellis
Designers Jan Ellis, Laurie Ellis
Photographer Mark Tucker
Studio Ellis Design
Client Athens Paper
Category Design/Single Page or Spread
Date July 1992

Publication Show Offs
Award Merit
Art Directors Jan Ellis, Laurie Ellis
Designers Jan Ellis, Laurie Ellis
Photographer Mark Tucker
Studio Ellis Design
Client Athens Paper
Category Design/Single Page or Spread
Date July 1992

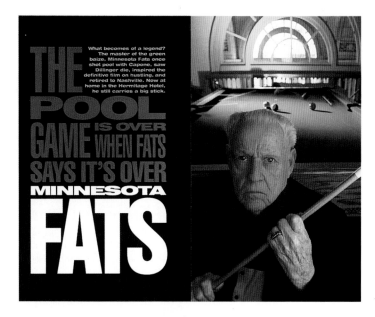

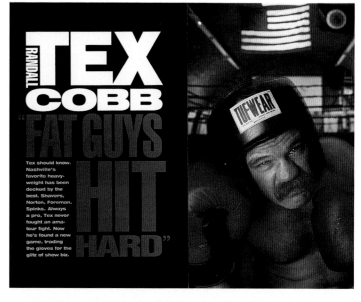

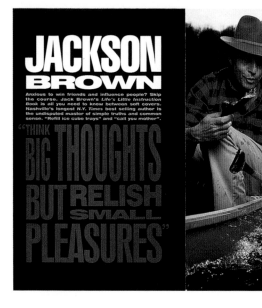

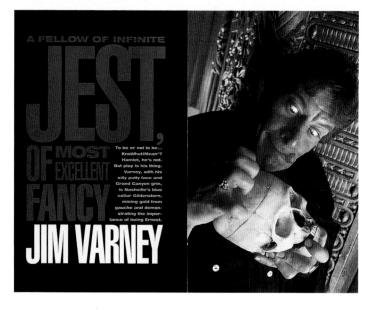

Publication Show Offs
Award Merit
Art Directors Jan Ellis, Laurie Ellis
Designers Jan Ellis, Laurie Ellis
Photographer Mark Tucker
Studio Ellis Design
Client Athens Paper
Category Design/Single Page or Spread
Date July 1992

Publication Show Offs
Award Merit
Art Directors Jan Ellis, Laurie Ellis
Designers Jan Ellis, Laurie Ellis
Photographer Mark Tucker
Studio Ellis Design
Client Athens Paper
Category Design/Single Page or Spread
Date July 1992

Publication Stanford Magazine
Award Merit
Art Director Paul Carstensen
Designer Paul Carstensen
Illustrator Glenn Matsumura
Photographer Glenn Matsumura
Publisher Stanford Alumni Association
Category Design/Single Page or Spread
Date December 1992

Publication Stanford Medicine
Award Merit
Art Director David Armario
Designer David Armario
Illustrator Terry Allen
Category Design/Single Page or Spread
Date Fall 1992

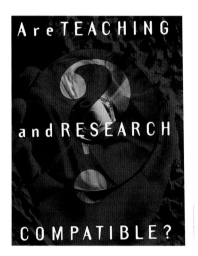

Publication World Tour
Award Merit
Design Director Gary Koepke
Art Director Gary Koepke
Designer Diddo Ramm
Studio Koepke Design Group
Category Design/Single Page or Spread
Date March 1992

Publication World Tour
Award Merit
Design Director Gary Koepke
Art Director Gary Koepke
Designer Diddo Ramm
Illustrator Isamu Noguchi
Studio Koepke Design Group
Category Design/Single Page or Spread
Date March 1992

Publication World Tour
Award Merit
Design Director Gary Koepke
Art Director Gary Koepke
Studio Koepke Design Group
Category Design/Single Page or Spread
Date March 1992

Publication World Tour
Award Merit
Design Director Gary Koepke
Art Director Gary Koepke
Designer Diddo Ramm
Illustrator Joseph Glidden
Studio Koepke Design Group
Category Design/Single Page or Spread
Date March 1992

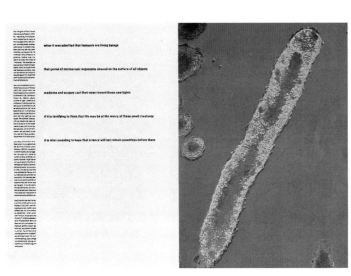

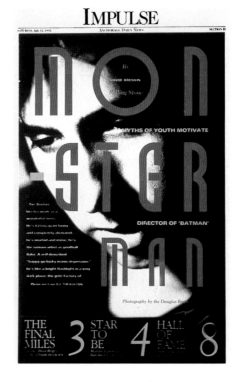

Publication World Tour
Award Merit
Design Director Gary Koepke
Art Director Gary Koepke
Designer Diddo Ramm
Photographers Henri Dauman/Magnum
Studio Koepke Design Group
Category Design/Single Page or Spread
Date March 1992

Publication Anchorage Daily News
Award Merit
Design Director Galie Jean-Louis
Art Director Galie Jean-Louis
Designer Galie Jean-Louis
Photographer The Douglas Brothers
Photo Editor Galie Jean-Louis
Publisher Anchorage Daily News
Category Design/Single Page or Spread
Date July 1992

Publication The Village Voice
Award Merit
Design Director Robert Newman
Designer Florian Bachleda
Photographer James Hamilton
Photo Editor Edna Suarez
Publisher Village Voice Publishing Corporation
Category Design/Single Page or Spread
Date November 1992

Publication Eastsideweek
Award Merit
Art Director Sandra Schneider
Photographer Mark Van-S
Publisher Sasquatch Publishing
Category Design/Single Page or Spread
Date December 16, 1992

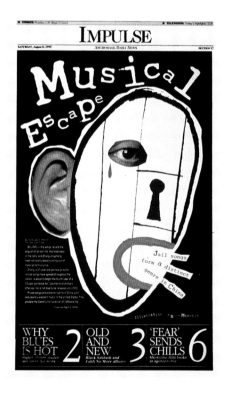

Publication Anchorage Daily News
Award Merit
Design Director Galie Jean-Louis
Art Director Galie Jean-Louis
Designer Galie Jean-Louis
Illustrator Scott Menchin
Publisher Anchorage Daily News
Category Design/Single Page or Spread
Date August 1992

Publication Eastsideweek
Award Merit
Art Director Sandra Schneider
Photographer Karen Moskowitz
Publisher Sasquatch Publishing
Category Design/Single Page or Spread
Date September 2, 1992

Publication	The Washington Times
Award	Merit
Design Director	Joseph W. Scopin
Art Director	John Kascht
Designer	John Kascht
Illustrator	John Kascht
Publisher	The Washington Times
Category	Design/Single Page or Spread
Date	February 9, 1992

Publication	The Washington Times
Award	Merit
Design Director	Joseph W. Scopin
Art Director	John Kascht
Designer	John Kascht
Illustrator	Don Asmussen
Publisher	The Washington Times
Category	Design/Single Page or Spread
Date	October 25, 1992

Publication	The Washington Times
Award	Merit
Design Director	Joseph W. Scopin
Art Director	John Kascht
Designer	John Kascht
Illustrator	John Kascht
Publisher	The Washington Times
Category	Design/Single Page or Spread
Date	November 1, 1992

Publication	The Washington Times
Award	Merit
Design Director	Joseph W. Scopin
Art Director	Dolores Motichka
Designer	Dolores Motichka
Illustrator	David Cowles
Publisher	The Washington Times
Category	Design/Single Page or Spread
Date	January 20, 1992

Publication The Boston Globe Magazine
Award Merit
Art Director Lucy Bartholomay
Designer Lucy Bartholomay
Illustrator J.W. Stewart
Publisher The Boston Globe Publishing Co.
Category Design/Single Page or Spread
Date October 11, 1992

Publication The Boston Globe/Special Section
Award Merit
Art Director Rena Sokolow
Designer Rena Sokolow
Illustrator Bob Hambly
Publisher The Boston Globe Publishing Co.
Category Design/Single Page or Spread
Date October 4, 1992

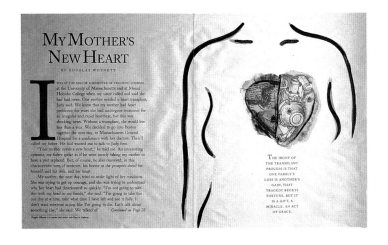

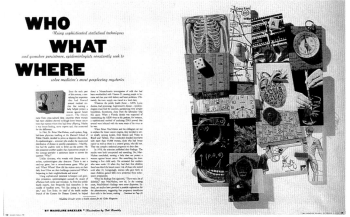

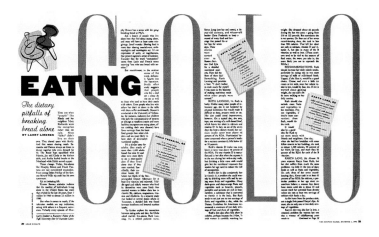

Publication The Boston Globe/Special Section
Award Merit
Art Director Rena Sokolow
Designer Rena Sokolow
Illustrator Anne Field
Publisher The Boston Globe Publishing Co.
Category Design/Single Page or Spread
Date October 4, 1992

Publication The Boston Globe Magazine
Award Merit
Art Director Lucy Bartholomay
Designer Lucy Bartholomay
Illustrator Patrick Blackwell
Publisher The Boston Globe Publishing Co.
Category Design/Single Page or Spread
Date July 5, 1992

Publication LA Times Magazine
Award Merit
Art Director Nancy Duckworth
Illustrator Keith Graves
Photo Editor Lisa Thackaberry
Publisher Los Angeles Times
Category Design/Single Page or Spread
Date November 1, 1992

Publication LA Times Magazine
Award Merit
Art Director Nancy Duckworth
Photographer Moshe Brakha
Photo Editor Lisa Thackaberry
Publisher Los Angeles Times
Category Design/Single Page or Spread
Date November 29, 1992

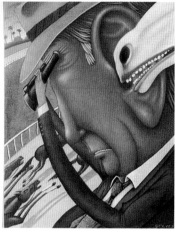
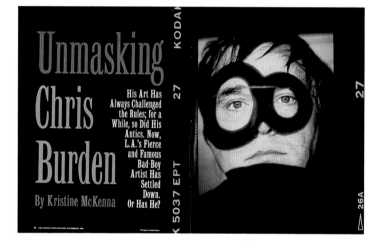

Publication The New York Times Magazine
Award Merit
Art Director Janet Froelich
Designer Kandy Littrell
Photographer Andrew Eccles
Photo Editor Kathy Ryan
Publisher The New York Times
Category Design/Single Page or Spread
Date May 31, 1992

Publication The New York Times Magazine
Award Merit
Art Director Janet Froelich
Designer Kathi Rota
Photographers Dan Winters, Eve Arnold
Photo Editor Kathy Ryan
Publisher The New York Times
Category Design/Single Page or Spread
Date October 25, 1992

Publication The New York Times Magazine
Award Merit
Art Director Janet Froelich
Designer Charlene Benson
Photo Editor Kathy Ryan
Publisher The New York Times
Category Design/Single Page or Spread
Date July 26, 1992

Publication The New York Times Magazine
Award Merit
Art Director Janet Froelich
Designer Kandy Littrell
Photographer Jon Jones
Photo Editor Kathy Ryan
Publisher The New York Times
Category Design/Single Page or Spread
Date July 26, 1992

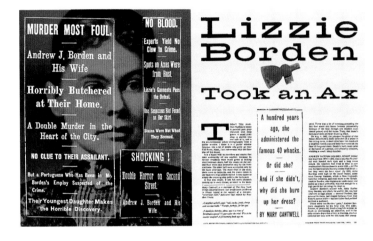

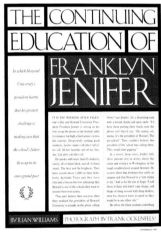

Publication The New York Times Magazine
Award Merit
Design Director Janet Froelich
Art Director Janet Froelich
Designer Holly Dickens
Photographer Geof Kern
Publisher The New York Times
Studio Holly Dickens Design
Category Design/Single Page or Spread
Date September 13, 1992

Publication The Washington Post Magazine
Award Merit
Art Director Richard Baker
Designer Richard Baker
Photographer Frank W. Ockenfels 3
Photo Editor Deborah Needleman
Publisher The Washington Post Co.
Category Design/Single Page or Spread
Date September 20, 1992

Publication	Rolling Stone
Award	Silver
Art Director	Fred Woodward
Designer	Fred Woodward
Photographer	Albert Watson
Photo Editor	Laurie Kratochvil
Publisher	Straight Arrow Publishers, Inc.
Category	Design/Story
Date	May 28, 1992

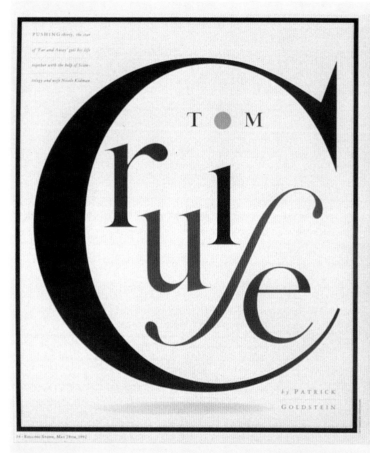

Publication Graphis
Award Silver
Design Director B. Martin Pedersen
Art Director Randell Pearson
Designer B. Martin Pedersen
Photographer Poul Ib Henriksen
Publisher Graphis US, Inc.
Category Design/Story
Date May/June 1992

BANG & OLUFSEN

Design STORY

Publication Digital News
Award Silver
Art Director Mark Koudys
Designer Mark Koudys
Photographer Ron Baxter Smith
Studio Atlanta Art & Design
Client Digital Equipment of Canada
Category Design/Story
Date November 1992

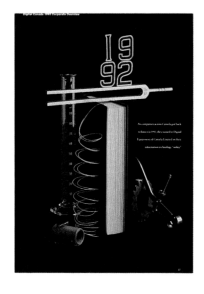

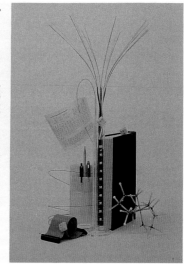

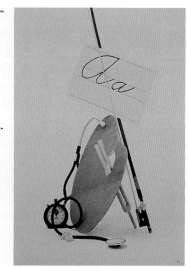

Publication Martha Stewart Living
Award Silver
Design Director Gael Towey
Art Director Anne Johnson
Photographers Victoria Pearson, Davies & Starr
Publisher Time Inc. Ventures
Category Design/Story
Date October/November 1992

apples *Old varieties rediscovered.*

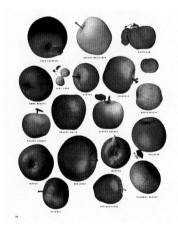

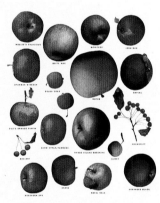

Publication	The Atlantic Monthly
Award	Merit
Design Director	Judy Garlan
Art Director	Judy Garlan
Designers	Judy Garlan, Robin Gilmore-Barnes
Illustrator	Karen Barbour
Publisher	The Atlantic Monthly
Category	Design/Story
Date	October 1992

Publication	Condé Nast Traveler
Award	Merit
Design Director	Diana LaGuardia
Art Director	Christin Gangi
Designer	Christin Gangi
Illustrator	John Grimwade
Photographer	Hakan Ludwigsson
Publisher	Condé Nast Publishing Co., Inc.
Category	Design/Story
Date	June 1992

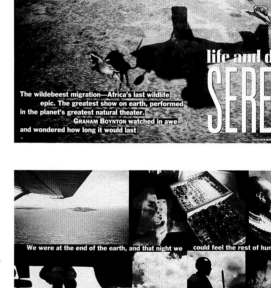

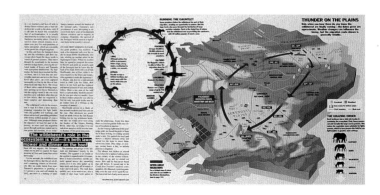

Publication Condé Nast Traveler
Award Merit
Design Director Diana LaGuardia
Art Director Christin Gangi
Designer Audrey Razgaitis
Photographer Richard Misrach
Publisher Condé Nast Publishing Co., Inc.
Category Design/Story
Date March 1992

Publication Entertainment Weekly
Award Merit
Design Director Michael Grossman
Art Director Mark Michaelson
Designer Mark Michaelson
Photographer Ruven Afanador
Photo Editors Mary Dunn, Doris Brautigan
Publisher Entertainment Weekly, Inc.
Category Design/Story
Date April 10, 1992

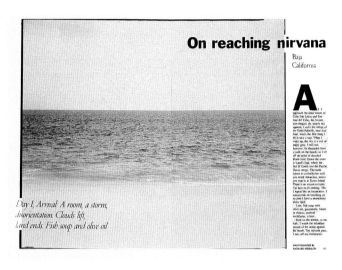

On reaching nirvana

Baja California

Day 1, Arrival: A room, a storm, disorientation. Clouds lift, land ends. Fish soup and olive oil

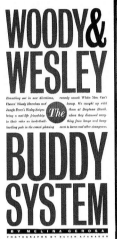

WOODY& WESLEY
The
BUDDY SYSTEM
BY MELINA GEROSA

Day 3, Acclimation: The passion next door: 10 A.M. Sublime pain. The languid passing of time

AT TIMES SNIPES AND HARRELSON ARE SO SIMILAR THEY SEEM LIKE EERIE DOUBLE-MINT TWINS

Day 2, Adjustment: Bleary dawn, patience, pelicans. A nap without time. Fragrance of lime. Shrimp.

"I FEEL 16 WHEN I'M WITH THIS GUY," SAYS HARRELSON. "MY FRIENDS CAN'T STAND ME WITH HIM," SNIPES SAYS.

Publication	Harper's Bazaar
Award	Merit
Creative Director	Fabien Baron
Art Director	Joel Berg
Designer	Johan Svensson
Photographer	Peter Lindbergh
Publisher	The Hearst Corporation
Category	Design/Story
Date	December 1992

Publication	Harper's Bazaar
Award	Merit
Creative Director	Fabien Baron
Art Director	Joel Berg
Designer	Johan Svensson
Photographer	Patrick Demarchelier
Publisher	The Hearst Corporation
Category	Design/Story
Date	November 1992

"**in my** solitude here, I have what is needed to recharge my forces. Here, poetry exudes from everywhere.... One has only to drift away into a dream to find inspiration."
—Paul Gauguin

Photographed by Peter Lindbergh

Out on the ocean, away from it all, still you always travel in style: all spare chic and unstudied glamour. This page: Yellow silk caftan, worn over matching silk slim pants, about $5960, the outfit by Bill Blass. Opposite page: White nylon Lycra maillot with thin spaghetti straps, about $egg, by Isaac Mizrahi. Eyeglasses, Robert Marc Opticians, NYC.

"I have escaped everything that is artificial and conventional. Here I enter into truth, become one with Nature." Opposite page: Long orange, green and red floral-motif dress of sequins on silk, about $5400, by Todd Oldham. Wanna have cleansed their skin with fruit for centuries. The modern spin: Alpha hydroxy acids, many derived from citrus fruits, give cosmetics miracle-working capabilities. Skin cells turn over more quickly, so complexions are smoother, younger- and brighter-looking. Products containing AHA include: Chanel's Day Lift Refining Complex, Avon's Anew Perfecting Complex, La Prairie's Age Management Serum, Elizabeth Arden's Time Complex Moisture Creme, Prescriptives' All You Need?, and, launching in February, Estée Lauder's Fruition Triple Reluxinating Complex.

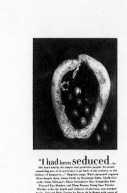

"I had been **seduced**... by this land and by its simple and primitive people. To create something new, it is necessary to go back to the sources, to the infancy of humanity...." Opposite page: White jacquard organza floor-length shirt, about $250, by Randolph Duke. Chalk-free Prescriptives Eye Shadow and Plum Bronze Young Face Powder blither echo the depth and richness of glorious, sun-warmed fruits. Valeyte Daily Lotion by Orcae de la Renta with scents of melon, citrus, and exotic flowers soothes and moisturizes, enveloping skin in the scent of tropical nights.

The bathing suit goes glamorous. Opposite page: Tango mini-strap bikini top, sold with matching bottoms, about $180, the set, by Laura Urbinati & Sara Marvini. Tango swimwear polo sweater, about $390, from J. Grow Collection. Santa Karan hat. This page: Light yellow bikini from J. Grow. This page bikini: Hair and styled by Madeleine Galtee for Frederic Fekkai at Bergdorf Goodman; makeup, Meisa Mulholland for the Olive Salon, NYC, and Fulvia Baroffi. Photographed aboard Pearl Yacht Line's Monatte, coordinated by La Maison la Vie, Saint Barthélemy. See Buyline for details and stores.

Publication	Harper's Bazaar
Award	Merit
Creative Director	Fabien Baron
Art Director	Joel Berg
Photographer	Peter Lindbergh
Publisher	The Hearst Corporation
Category	Design/Story
Date	September 1992

Publication	Harper's Bazaar
Award	Merit
Creative Director	Fabien Baron
Art Director	Joel Berg
Designer	Johan Svensson
Photographer	Peter Lindbergh
Publisher	The Hearst Corporation
Category	Design/Story
Date	November 1992

Redefining the boundaries of fashion: the season's important, impeccable menswear looks, and the brilliant contradiction of women who claim tailoring as their own, not in emulation, but for its straightforward manner, its ability to take forms as studied, or abandoned, as the impulses of the wearer.

No Man's Land

Spirits of the night

CUT ON THE CROSS

Who's afraid of women in menswear? At the office, it may be our new statement of no surrender.
By Sarah Mower

Publication	Harper's Bazaar
Award	Merit
Creative Director	Fabien Baron
Art Director	Joel Berg
Photographer	Patrick Demarchelier
Publisher	The Hearst Corporation
Category	Design/Story
Date	September 1992

Publication	Hemispheres
Award	Merit
Design Director	Kit Hinrichs
Art Directors	Kit Hinrichs, Jaimey Easler
Designer	Jackie Foshaug
Illustrator	Andy Goldsworth
Photographer	Andy Goldsworth
Publisher	Pace Communications
Studio	Pentagram Design
Client	United Airlines
Category	Design/Story
Date	October 1992

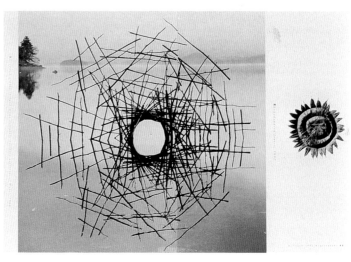

Publication	Life
Award	Merit
Design Director	Tom Bentkowski
Art Director	Nora Sheehan
Designer	Nora Sheehan
Photographer	Art Rogers
Photo Editor	Barbara Baker Burrows
Publisher	Time Inc. Magazine Company
Category	Design/Story
Date	June 1992

Publication	Life
Award	Merit
Design Director	Tom Bentkowski
Designer	Tom Bentkowski
Photographers	Paul Schutzer, Bill Ray, Harry Benson, Ed Caraeff, David Gahr, Annie Lebowitz, Lynn Goldsmith, Bruce Weber, Neal Preston
Publisher	Time/Warner, Inc.
Category	Design/Story
Date	December 1992

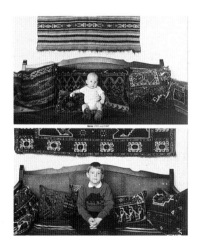

Publication	Martha Stewart Living
Award	Merit
Design Director	Gael Towey
Art Director	Laura Harrigan
Photographers	William Abranowicz, Maria Robledo
Publisher	Time Publishing Ventures
Category	Design/Story
Date	August/September 1992

Publication	Martha Stewart Living
Award	Merit
Design Director	Gael Towey
Art Director	Anne Johnson
Photographer	Maria Robledo
Publisher	Time Publishing Ventures
Category	Design/Story
Date	April/May 1992

POTATOES

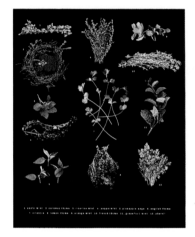

herbs

Publication Martha Stewart Living
Award Merit
Design Director Gael Towey
Art Director Jennifer Warerek
Photographer Bruce Wolf
Publisher Time Publishing Ventures
Category Design/Story
Date April/May 1992

Publication Metropolis
Award Merit
Art Directors Carl Lehmann-Haupt, Nancy Cohen, Kevin Slavin
Designers Carl Lehmann-Haupt, Nancy Cohen
Photographer Jill Greenberg
Publisher Bellerophon Publications, Inc.
Category Design/Story
Date October 1992

PAINT-ING THE

HOUSE

PHOTOGRAPHS BY BRUCE WOLF

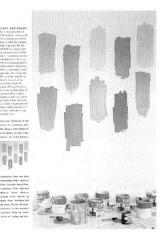

america

?

edited by Karrie Jacobs

What one object represents the epitome of American design? That's what we asked randomly chosen design professionals from 50 states and dozens of countries. We hoped that their responses would help us assemble a portrait of American design today. What we learned is that the designers, like politicians, still seek their ideals in the past.

Rising from the edge of Lake Michigan, 860 and 880 Lake Shore Drive in Chicago have been called the "best known monuments of post-war American architecture. Naturally, they were designed by an emigré. by Janet Abrams

modernity

guggenheim museum

philip johnson's glass house

richard neutra's lovell house

tastelessness

Great European design is almost always based on one aesthetic theory or another. Great American design is almost always based on the studied disregard of aesthetic theory. by Constantin Boym

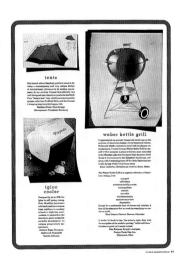

tents

weber kettle grill

igloo cooler

Publication	Metropolis
Award	Merit
Art Directors	Carl Lehmann-Haupt, Nancy Cohen
Designers	Carl Lehmann-Haupt, Nancy Cohen
Illustrator	Chip Kidd
Photographers	Dan Winters, Benita Raphan
Publisher	Bellerophon Publications, Inc.
Category	Design/Story
Date	May 1992

Publication	Metropolis
Award	Merit
Art Directors	Carl Lehmann-Haupt, Nancy Cohen
Designers	Carl Lehmann-Haupt, Nancy Cohen
Photographer	Bruce Osborne
Publisher	Bellerophon Publications, Inc.
Category	Design/Story
Date	September 1992

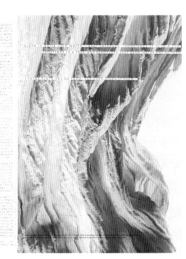

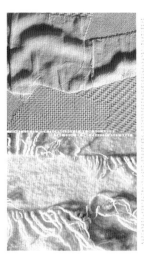

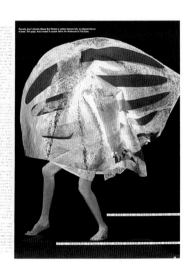

Publication	Natur
Award	Merit
Art Directors	Christof Gassner, Fabian Nicolay
Designer	Christof Gassner
Photo Editor	Jurgen Fahrenholz
Publisher	Ringier Verlag GMbH
Category	Design/Story
Date	July 1992

Publication	Popular Science
Award	Merit
Art Director	W. David Houser
Designer	W. Thomas White
Publisher	Times Mirror
Category	Design/Story
Date	August 1992

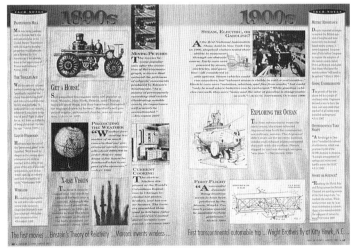

Publication	Sports Illustrated
Award	Merit
Design Director	Steven Hoffman
Designer	Craig Gartner
Photographer	Chuck Solomon
Photo Editor	Karen Mullarkey
Publisher	Time Inc. Magazine Company
Category	Design/Story
Date	April 1992

Publication	SPY
Award	Merit
Art Director	Christiaan Kuypers
Designers	Daniel Carter, Damon Torres
Photo Editor	Nicki Gostin
Publisher	SPY Corporation
Category	Design/Story
Date	November 1992

Publication	Texas Monthly
Award	Merit
Design Director	D.J. Stout
Art Director	D.J. Stout
Designer	D.J. Stout
Photographer	Geof Kern
Photo Editor	D.J. Stout
Publisher	Texas Monthly
Category	Design/Story
Date	July 1992

Publication	Texas Monthly
Award	Merit
Design Director	D.J. Stout
Art Director	D.J. Stout
Designer	D.J. Stout
Photographer	Keith Carter
Photo Editor	D.J. Stout
Publisher	Texas Monthly
Category	Design/Story
Date	January 1992

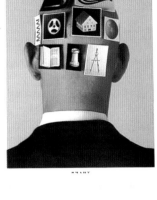

135

Publication	Texas Monthly
Award	Merit
Design Director	D.J. Stout
Art Director	D.J. Stout
Designer	D.J. Stout
Photographer	Dan Winters
Photo Editor	D.J. Stout
Publisher	Texas Monthly
Category	Design/Story
Date	June 1992

Publication	Texas Monthly
Award	Merit
Design Director	D.J. Stout
Art Director	D.J. Stout
Designer	D.J. Stout
Photographer	Mary Ellen Mark
Photo Editor	D.J. Stout
Publisher	Texas Monthly
Category	Design/Story
Date	March 1992

Meet the *Beetles*

AND OTHER AMAZING INSECTS THAT CALL TEXAS HOME

Photographs by DAN WINTERS
Text by Chris Dorden

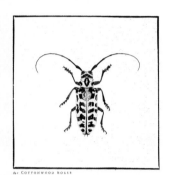

fig 1 COTTONWOOD BORER
Plectrodera scalator

fig 2 TROPICAL OX BEETLE
Strategus aloeus

fig 3 GIANT WALKINGSTICK
Megaphasma dentricus

fig 4 VINE SPHINX
Eumorpha vitis

fig 5 GROUND BEETLE
Pasimachus sublaevis punctulatus

fig 6 EYED CLICK BEETLE
Alaus lusciosus

fig 7 CICADA KILLER
Sphecius speciosus

fig 8 TWO-TAILED TIGER SWALLOWTAIL
Pterourus multicaudatus

RODEO TEXAS U★S★A PHOTO GRAPHY MARY ELLEN MARK

HERE'S TO THE SMALL-TOWN RODEO —PART CONTEST, PART PAGEANT, PART HARD KNOCKS AND HARD TRUTHS.

BY SKIP HOLLANDSWORTH

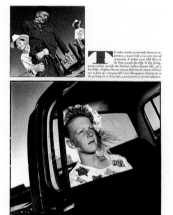

Publication	Time
Award	Merit
Design Director	Arthur Hochstein
Art Director	Rudolph C. Hoglund
Photographers	Department of Special Collections, Syracuse University Library; Courtesy of Margaret Bourke-White Estate., Juau/Black Star
Publisher	Time/Warner, Inc.
Category	Design/Story
Date	December 7, 1992

Publication	Travel Holiday
Award	Merit
Art Director	Lou DiLorenzo
Designers	Lou DiLorenzo, Jane Frey
Photographers	Dennis Marsico
Photo Editor	Bill Black
Publisher	Readers Digest Publications
Category	Design/Story
Date	November 1992

THE NEW RUSSIA / VIEWS
DEATH OF THE DREAM

Not much is different for the young boy building a blast furnace in the Russia of 60 years ago and the youthful coke oven tender who labors in the same factory today

WINTER in TUSCANY

by SAUL BELLOW — photographed by DENNIS MARSICO

The soils of all these fields seemed to have passed through millions of human hands.

Scanning the pope's huge leatherbound books, I wonder how one could have read them in bed.

Publication	Vibe	**Publication**	Us
Award	Merit	**Award**	Merit
Design Director	Gary Koepke	**Art Director**	Pamela Berry
Art Director	Gary Koepke	**Designer**	Sarika Aggarwal
Designer	Diddo Ramm	**Photographer**	Lance Staedler
Photographer	Albert Watson	**Photo Editor**	Thea Wieseltier Fattal
Studio	Koepke Design Group	**Publisher**	Straight Arrow Publishers
Category	Design/Story	**Category**	Design/Story
Date	Preveiw 1992	**Date**	January 1992

Publication Architectural Record
Award Merit
Design Director Alberto Bucchianeri
Designer Alberto Bucchianeri
Photographers Steve Hall, Hendrich- Blessing
Publisher McGraw-Hill Publications
Category Design/Story
Date January 1992

Publication Architectural Record
Award Merit
Design Director Alberto Bucchianeri
Designer Anna Egger-Schlesinger
Photographer Thomas Heinser
Publisher McGraw-Hill Publications
Category Design/Story
Date April 1992

Religious Conversion

The former United Hebrew Temple is born again as a research center for the Missouri Historical Society

Industrial Arts

Celebrating the beauty of rugged materials well connected, Richard Stacy has designed a slender structure that provides living and work space for two artists.

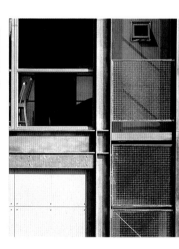

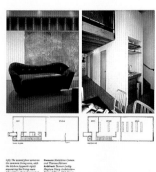

Publication	Architectural Record
Award	Merit
Design Director	Alberto Bucchianeri
Designer	Anna Egger-Schlesinger
Photographer	Ian Lambot
Publisher	McGraw-Hill Publications
Category	Design/Story
Date	June 1992

Publication	Forbes FYI
Award	Merit
Art Director	Alexander Isley
Designer	Lynette Cortez
Photographer	Monica Stevenson
Publisher	Forbes, Inc.
Studio	Alexander Isley Design
Category	Design/Story
Date	September 1992

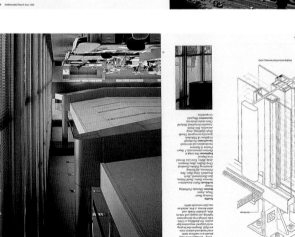

Publication	Forbes FYI
Award	Merit
Art Director	Alexander Isley
Designer	Kay Schuckhart
Illustrator	Roy Pendleton
Photographers	The Bettmann Archive
Publisher	Forbes, Inc.
Studio	Alexander Isley Design
Category	Design/Story
Date	1992

Publication	Graphis
Award	Merit
Design Director	B. Martin Pedersen
Art Directors	B. Martin Pedersen, Randell Pearson
Designer	B. Martin Pedersen
Publisher	Graphis US, Inc.
Category	Design/Story
Date	November/December 1992

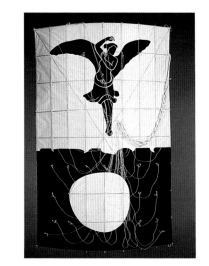

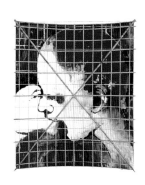

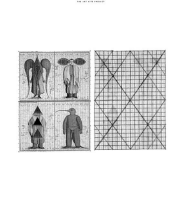

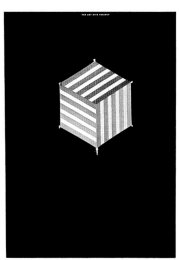

Publication	Graphis
Award	Merit
Design Director	B. Martin Pedersen
Art Directors	B. Martin Pedersen, Randell Pearson
Designer	B. Martin Pedersen
Publisher	Graphis US, Inc.
Category	Design/Story
Date	November/December 1992

Publication	Graphis
Award	Merit
Design Director	B. Martin Pedersen
Art Directors	B. Martin Pedersen, Randell Pearson
Designer	B. Martin Pedersen
Photographer	Masaru Mera
Publisher	Graphis US, Inc.
Category	Design/Story
Date	January/Feburary 1992

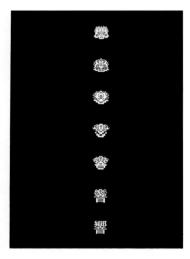

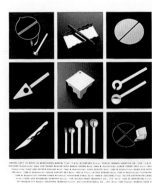

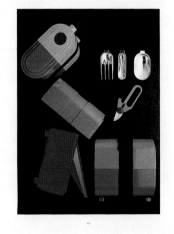

Publication	Graphis
Award	Merit
Design Director	B. Martin Pedersen
Art Directors	B. Martin Pedersen, Randell Pearson
Designer	B. Martin Pedersen
Photographer	Hiro
Publisher	Graphis US, Inc.
Category	Design/Story
Date	March/April 1992

Publication	Graphis
Award	Merit
Design Director	B. Martin Pedersen
Art Directors	B. Martin Pedersen, Randell Pearson
Designer	B. Martin Pedersen
Photographer	Michelle Clement
Publisher	Graphis US, Inc.
Category	Design/Story
Date	May/June 1992

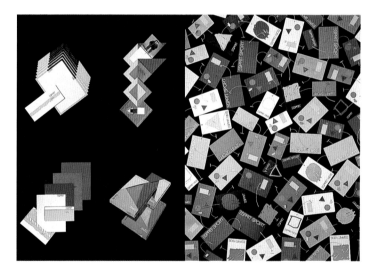

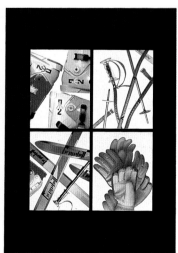

Publication	Graphis
Award	Merit
Design Director	B. Martin Pedersen
Art Directors	B. Martin Pedersen, Randell Pearson
Designer	B. Martin Pedersen
Photographer	Monica Lee
Publisher	Graphis US, Inc.
Category	Design/Story
Date	November/December 1992

Publication	U &lc
Award	Merit
Design Director	Milton Glaser
Art Director	Walter Bernard
Designers	Frank Baseman, Sharon Okamoto
Photographer	Matthew Klein
Studio	WBMG, Inc.
Category	Design/Story
Date	Spring 1992

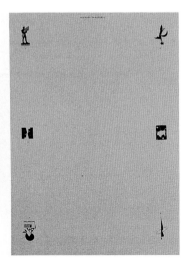

Publication	Digital News
Award	Merit
Design Director	Mark Koudys
Designer	Mark Koudys
Photographer	Ron Baker Smith
Client	Digital Equipment of Canada
Studio	Atlanta Art and Design
Category	Design/Story
Date	August 1992

Publication	Stanford Magazine
Award	Merit
Art Director	Paul Carstensen
Designer	Paul Carstensen
Photographer	Jason Langer
Publisher	Stanford Alumni Association
Category	Design/Story
Date	September 1992

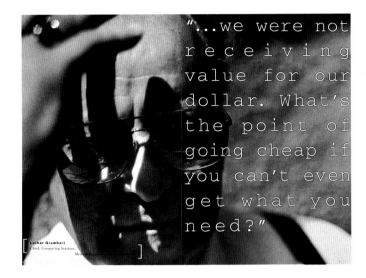

"...we were not receiving value for our dollar. What's the point of going cheap if you can't even get what you need?"

[Lothar Grambart
Chief, Computing Services]

An Atlas of the Difficult World: The Poetry Of Adrienne Rich

Gary D. Cardiff, CEO
[Ernie Zwarts, Director of Information Services]

Children's Hospital of Eastern Ontario

"It's all very well to have the boxes blinking away on desks or in the computer room, but the ease of communication and planning made possible by ALL-IN-1 is what makes our system truly powerful, for everyone."

The Poetry of Adrienne Rich

"The only way to stay competitive is to have the technology to make information available."

[Dave Binder
Manager of Computer Operations,
Gabhall Technologies Inc.]

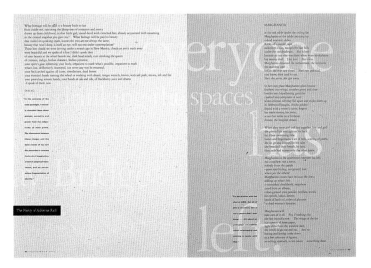

Design STORY

<table>
<tr><td>Publication</td><td>World</td><td>Publication</td><td>The New York Times Magazine</td></tr>
<tr><td>Award</td><td>Merit</td><td>Award</td><td>Merit</td></tr>
<tr><td>Art Director</td><td>Donna Bonavita</td><td>Art Director</td><td>Janet Froelich</td></tr>
<tr><td>Designer</td><td>Donna Bonavita</td><td>Designer</td><td>Kandy Littrell</td></tr>
<tr><td>Photographers</td><td>John Isaac, Kay Chernush, Jim Richardson, Terrance Moore, Suzi Moore, David Turnley</td><td>Photographer</td><td>Michael O'Brien</td></tr>
<tr><td></td><td></td><td>Publisher</td><td>The New York Times</td></tr>
<tr><td>Publisher</td><td>KPMG Peat Marwick, Communications Group</td><td>Category</td><td>Design/Story</td></tr>
<tr><td>Category</td><td>Design/Story</td><td>Date</td><td>July 5, 1992</td></tr>
<tr><td>Date</td><td>May 1992</td><td></td><td></td></tr>
</table>

Publication	The New York Times Magazine
Award	Merit
Art Director	Janet Froelich
Designer	Kathi Rota
Photographer	Danielle Well
Photo Editor	Kathy Ryan
Publisher	The New York Times
Category	Design/Story
Date	March 8, 1992

Publication	The New York Times Magazine
Award	Merit
Art Director	Janet Froelich
Designers	Kathi Rota, Kandy Littrell
Illustrators	John Collier, David Sandlin, Ross MacDonald, Gary Panter, Anthony Russo
Publisher	The New York Times
Category	Design/Story
Date	December 25, 1992

BASEBALL

Playing the Angles and Going Down the Lines • A Photo Essay by Danielle Weil • Text by David Halberstam

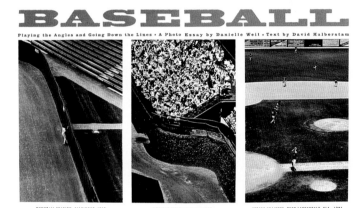

MEMORIAL STADIUM, BALTIMORE, 1965 • WRIGLEY FIELD, CHICAGO, 1966 • SPRING TRAINING, FORT LAUDERDALE, FLA., 1961

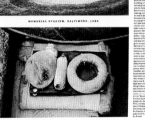

FENWAY PARK, BOSTON, 1990 • MEMORIAL STADIUM, BALTIMORE, 1990 • SHEA STADIUM, NEW YORK, 1990 • BATTING STUFF, MEMORIAL STADIUM, BALTIMORE, 1990

Christmas Observed

No Tracks In the Snow

ILLUSTRATION BY JOHN COLLIER

Crossing The Line

ILLUSTRATION BY DAVID SANDLIN

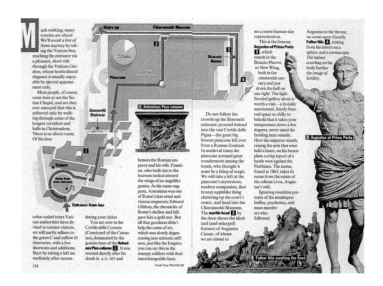

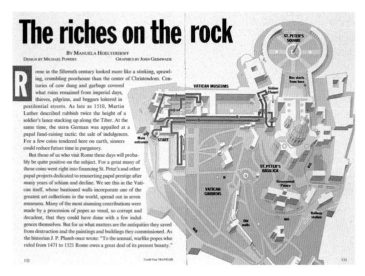

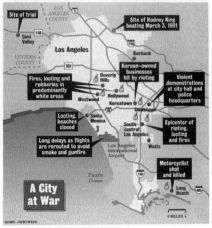

Publication Condé Nast Traveler
Award Merit
Design Director Diana La Guardia
Art Director Christin Gangi
Designer Mike Powers
Illustrator John Grimwade
Publisher Condé Nast Publishing Co., Inc.
Category Information Graphics
Date April 1992

Publication Newsweek
Award Merit
Art Director Patricia Bradbury
Designer Dixon Rohr
Publisher Newsweek, Inc.
Category Information Graphics
Date May 11, 1992

Publication Entertainment Weekly
Award Merit
Design Director Michael Grossman
Art Director Arlene Lappen
Designer Michael Picón
Photo Editor Mary Dunn
Publisher Entertainment Weekly, Inc.
Category Information Graphics
Date August 14, 1992

Publication Entertainment Weekly
Award Merit
Design Director Michael Grossman
Art Director Mark Michaelson
Designer Michael Grossman
Illustrator Barry Blitt
Photographers Sylvia Otte, Anthony Verde
Photo Editors Mary Dunn, Michelle Romero
Publisher Entertainment Weekly, Inc.
Category Information Graphics
Date March 20, 1992

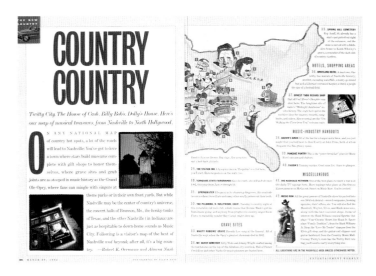

Publication Condé Nast Traveler
Award Merit
Design Director Diana La Guardia
Art Director Christin Gangi
Designer Christin Gangi
Illustrators John Grimwade, Greg
Wakabayashi
Publisher Condé Nast Publishing Co., Inc.
Category Information Graphics
Date December 1992

Publication Kids Discover
Award Merit
Design Directors Will Hopkins, Mary K. Baumann
Illustrator Paul M. Breeden
Photo Editor Fay Torresyap
Publisher Kids Discover
Studio Hopkins/Baumann
Category Information Graphics
Date August/September 1992

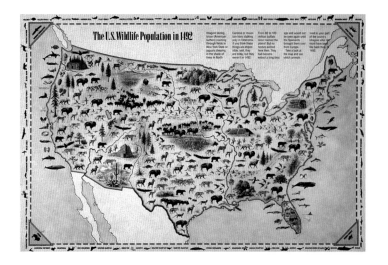

Publication Fortune
Award Merit
Art Director Margery Peters
Designer Tony Mikolajczyk
Publisher Time Inc. Magazine Group
Category Information Graphics
Date August 1992

Publication Newsweek
Award Merit
Art Director Patricia Bradbury
Designer Dixon Rohr
Publisher Newsweek, Inc.
Category Information Graphics
Date June 1, 1992

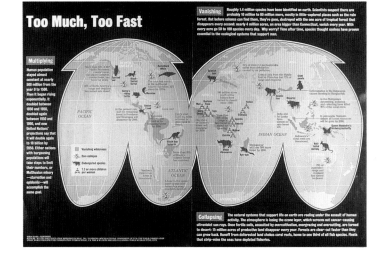

25 Traveler's
islands to call your own

PRIVATE ISLANDS ARE THE ULTIMATE IN exclusivity. You may not be as rich as Onassis, but an island you are—a virtual monarch, reigning from shore to shore. Privately owned islands come in all sizes and shapes, from tiny, four-bedroom Chauve Souris in Seychelles, to 35-acre Young Island in the Caribbean, to Waterford Castle off the coast of Ireland. On the following pages, JENNIFER CECIL reports from 25 privately owned islands with guest facilities and a variety of features (see key below). Some are pure tropical getaways, others are nature preserves, still others are havens for scuba divers or golfers, some are luxurious, others are simple, and on some you can rent the entire island—achieving total solitude, if not absolute monarchy.

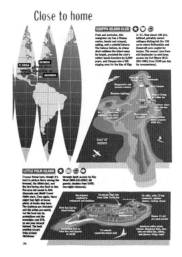

Close to home

Publication — Condé Nast Traveler
Award — Merit
Design Director — Diana La Guardia
Designer — Christin Gangi
Illustrators — John Grimwade, Greg Wakabayashi
Publisher — Condé Nast Publishing Co., Inc.
Category — Information Graphics
Date — September 1992

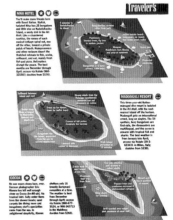

The Indian Ocean: Pizza and divemasters

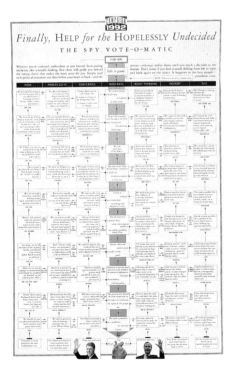

Publication — SPY
Award — Merit
Art Director — Christiaan Kuypers
Designers — Daniel Carter, Damon Torres
Publisher — SPY Corporation
Category — Information Graphics
Date — November 1992

Publication — Computerworld
Award — Merit
Design Director — Nancy Kowal
Illustrator — Hal Mayforth
Publisher — C.W. Publishing, Inc.
Category — Information Graphics
Date — December 1992

ILLUSTRATION

single page

SPREAD

Story

Publication The Washington Post Magazine
Award Gold
Art Director Richard Baker
Designer Richard Baker
Illustrator Geof Kern
Photo Editor Deborah Needleman
Publisher The Washington Post Co.
Category Illustration/Single Page or Spread
Date November 15, 1992

EXECUTIVE GROOMING 101

I

In this introductory course, Professor Glenn Pfau will instruct students on exactly what it takes to be a successful executive in America today. Thin soles and analog watches required By Jeanne Marie Laskas

There is no creature whose inward being is so strong that it is not greatly determined by what lies outside it.
—George Eliot

am thinking about inward versus outward beings as I sit through the opening hours of "Projecting a Positive Executive Image," course No. 2274-202 at the American Management Association's Washington center on First Street NW. This is a two-day executive grooming seminar intended to teach you the ways of corporate America, so that you can blend in, become accepted and climb the ladder leading ever up-

PHOTO ILLUSTRATIONS BY GEOF KERN

NOVEMBER 15, 1992   15

Publication Sports Illustrated
Award Silver
Design Director Steven Hoffman
Designer F. Darrin Perry
Illustrator Anastasia Vasilakis
Publisher Time Inc. Magazine Company
Category Illustration/Single Page or Spread
Date November 16, 1992

Blood Money

In the rich, clubby world of horsemen, some greedy owners have hired killers to murder their animals for the insurance payoffs | by WILLIAM NACK and LESTER MUNSON

O N THE RAINY NIGHT OF Feb. 2, 1991, in despair over the prospect of causing the death of a horse by breaking its hind leg with a crowbar, Tommy (the Sandman) Burns sat in a bar outside Gainesville, Fla., and got drunk on gin and tonic. "Really wasted," Burns recalls. "I had never done one like that before." ■ For a decade the chunky 30-year-old had made a sporadic living as a hit man hired to destroy expensive horses and ponies, usually so their owners could collect on lucrative life-insurance policies. But no owner had ever ordered Burns to dispose of a horse by breaking one of its legs—that is, by causing a trauma so severe that a veterinarian would be forced to put the animal down with a lethal injection. ■ Burns's preferred method of killing horses was electrocution. It had been so ever since the day in 1982 when, he says, the late James Druck, an Ocala, Fla., attorney who represented insurance companies, paid him to kill the brilliant show jumper Henry the Hawk, on whose life Druck had taken out a $150,000 life-insurance policy. In fact, says Burns, Druck personally taught him how to rig the wires to electrocute Henry the Hawk: how to slice an extension cord down the middle into two strands of wire; how to attach a pair of alligator clips to the bare end of each wire; and how to attach the

Publication Abitare
Award Merit
Design Director Italo Lupi
Art Director Italo Lupi
Designer Italo Lupi
Illustrator Steven Guarnaccia
Publisher Abitare
Studio Steven Guarnaccia
Category Illustration/Single Page or Spread
Date July/August 1992

Publication Abitare
Award Merit
Design Director Italo Lupi
Art Director Italo Lupi
Designer Italo Lupi
Illustrator Steven Guarnaccia
Publisher Abitare
Studio Steven Guarnaccia
Category Illustration/Single Page or Spread
Date May 1992

Publication Abitare
Award Merit
Design Director Italo Lupi
Art Director Italo Lupi
Designer Italo Lupi
Illustrator Steven Guarnaccia
Publisher Abitare
Studio Steven Guarnaccia
Category Illustration/Single Page or Spread
Date March 1992

Publication The Atlantic Monthly
Award Merit
Design Director Judy Garlan
Art Director Judy Garlan
Designer Judy Garlan
Illustrator Gary Kelley
Publisher The Atlantic Monthly
Category Illustration/Single Page or Spread
Date September 1992

Publication	Details
Award	Merit
Art Director	B.W. Honeycutt
Illustrator	Jonathon Rosen
Publisher	Condé Nast Publishing Co., Inc.
Studio	Jonathon Rosen
Category	Illustration/Single Page or Spread
Date	August 1992

Publication	Entertainment Weekly
Award	Merit
Design Director	Michael Grossman
Art Director	Arlene Lappen
Designer	Michael Picón
Illustrator	Josh Gosfield
Publisher	Entertainment Weekly, Inc.
Category	Illustration/Single Page or Spread
Date	July 31, 1992

Publication	Esquire
Award	Merit
Art Director	Rhonda Rubinstein
Designer	Rhonda Rubinstein
Illustrator	Jeffrey Fisher
Publisher	The Hearst Corporation
Category	Illustration/Single Page or Spread
Date	January 1992

Publication GQ
Award Merit
Creative Director Robert Priest
Art Director Janet Parker
Designer Janet Parker
Illustrator Charles Burns
Publisher Condé Nast Publications
Category Illustration/Single Page or Spread
Date December 1992

Publication GQ
Award Merit
Creative Director Robert Priest
Designer Diana Haas
Illustrator Matt Mahurin
Photo Editor Karen Frank
Publisher Condé Nast Publications
Category Illustration/Single Page or Spread
Date September 1992

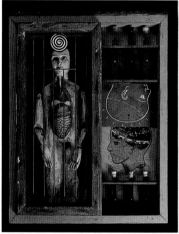

Publication Health
Award Merit
Art Director Jane Palecek
Designer Dorothy Marschall
Illustrator Gary Tanhauser.
Publisher Health
Category Illustration/Single Page or Spread
Date September 1992

Publication Health
Award Merit
Art Director Jane Palecek
Designer Dorothy Marschall
Illustrator Gary Tanhauser
Publisher Health
Category Illustration/Single Page or Spread
Date November/December 1992

Publication	Ray Gun
Award	Merit
Art Director	David Carson
Designer	David Carson
Illustrator	Jonathon Rosen
Publisher	Ray Gun
Studio	David Carson Design
Category	Illustration/Single Page or Spread
Date	December 1992

Publication	Playboy
Award	Merit
Art Director	Tom Staebler
Designer	Kelly Korjenek
Illustrator	David Wilcox
Publisher	Playboy
Category	Illustration/Single Page or Spread
Date	October 1992

Publication	Rolling Stone
Award	Merit
Art Director	Fred Woodward
Illustrator	Charles Burns
Publisher	Straight Arrow Publishers, Inc.
Category	Illustration/Single Page or Spread
Date	November 26, 1992

Publication Rolling Stone
Award Merit
Art Director Fred Woodward
Illustrator Sue Coe
Publisher Straight Arrow Publishers, Inc.
Category Illustration/Single Page or Spread
Date September 17, 1992

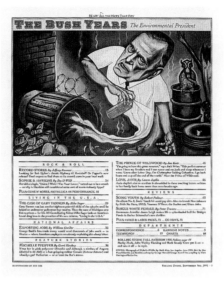

Publication Rolling Stone
Award Merit
Art Director Fred Woodward
Designers Fred Woodward, Gail Anderson,
Catherine Gilmore-Barnes,
Debra Bishop,
Angela Skouras, Geraldine Hessler
Illustrator Charles Burns
Publisher Straight Arrow Publishers, Inc.
Category Illustration/Single Page or Spread
Date October 15, 1992

Publication San Francisco Focus
Award Merit
Art Director Mark Ulriksen
Designer Anita Wong
Illustrator Barry Blitt
Publisher KQED, Inc.
Category Illustration/Single Page or Spread
Date May 1992

Publication	Special Report
Award	Merit
Art Directors	Doug Renfro, Jim Phillips
Designer	Julie Schrader
Illustrator	Silvia Taccani
Publisher	Whittle Communications
Category	Illustration/Single Page or Spread
Date	November/December 1992

Publication	Sports Illustrated
Award	Merit
Design Director	Steven Hoffman
Art Director	F. Darrin Perry
Designer	F. Darrin Perry
Illustrator	Josh Gosfield
Publisher	Time Inc. Magazine Company
Category	Illustration/Single Page or Spread
Date	Fall 1992

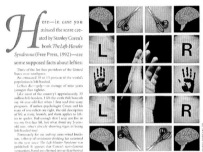

MY LEFT HAND

Do southpaws—ahem—go south sooner?

The
Last
Remains
of a
Legend

Ty Cobb, baseball's eccentric genius, died in rural Georgia more than 30 years ago, very wealthy and virtually alone. The author recently paid him a visit

by Leigh Montville

Illustrations by Josh Gosfield

Publication	Forbes FYI
Award	Merit
Art Director	Alexander Isley
Designer	Lyneete Cortez
Illustrator	C.F. Payne
Publisher	Forbes, Inc.
Studio	Alexander Isley Design
Category	Illustration/Single Page or Spread
Date	May 1992

Seven word processors
that polish your prose—
and more

BEYOND
WORDS

BY GENE McCLELLAND

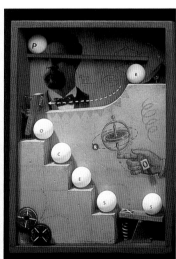

PHOTO ILLUSTRATIONS
BY GARY TANHAUSER

Publication	Macworld
Award	Merit
Design Director	Dennis McLeod
Art Director	Joanne Hoffman
Designer	Tim Johnson
Illustrator	Gary Tanhauser
Publisher	Macworld Communications
Category	Illustration/Single Page or Spread
Date	September 1992

Publication Wordperfect For Windows
Award Merit
Art Director Ron Stucki
Designer Kate Johnson
Illustrator John Craig
Publisher Wordperfect Publishing
Category Illustration/Single Page or Spread
Date December 1992

Publication Stanford Magazine
Award Merit
Art Director Paul Carstensen
Designer Paul Carstensen
Illustrator Amy Guip
Publisher Stanford Alumni Association
Category Illustration/Single Page or Spread
Date December 1992

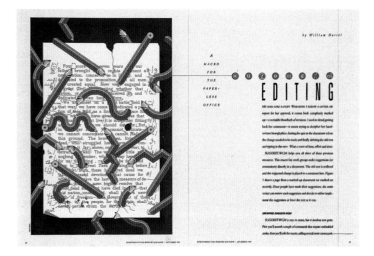

Publication Stanford Medicine
Award Merit
Art Director David Armario
Designer David Armario
Illustrator Terry Allen
Category Illustration/Single Page or Spread
Date Fall 1992

Publication The Village Voice
Award Merit
Design Director Robert Newman
Designer John Dinglasan
Illustrator Stephen Kroninger
Publisher Village Voice Publishing Corporation
Category Illustration/Single Page or Spread
Date April 1992

Publication The Village Voice
Award Merit
Design Director Robert Newman
Designer Jennifer Gilman
Illustrator Frances Jetter
Publisher Village Voice Publishing Corporation
Category Illustration/Single Page or Spread
Date May 19, 1992

Publication The Village Voice
Award Merit
Design Director Robert Newman
Designer Florian Bachleda
Illustrator Steve Brodner
Publisher Village Voice Publishing Corporation
Category Illustration/Single Page or Spread
Date June 9, 1992

Publication The Wall Street Journal Reports
Award Merit
Design Director Greg Leeds
Designer Greg Leeds
Illustrator Thomas Kerr
Publisher Dow Jones & Co., Inc.
Category Illustration/Single Page or Spread
Date September 21, 1992

Publication The Boston Globe Magazine
Award Merit
Art Director Lucy Bartholomay
Designer Lucy Bartholomay
Illustrator Joseph Daniel Fiedler
Publisher The Boston Globe Publishing Co.
Category Illustration/Single Page or Spread
Date May 10, 1992

Publication The New York Times Magazine
Award Merit
Art Director Janet Froelich
Designer Kandy Littrell
Illustrator Steven Guarnaccia
Publisher The New York Times
Category Illustration/Single Page or Spread
Date March 1, 1992

Publication The Philadelphia Inquirer Magazine
Award Merit
Design Director Jessica Helfand
Art Director Bert Fox
Designer Jessica Helfand
Illustrator Scott Menchin
Publisher The Philadelphia Inquirer
Category Illustration/Single Page or Spread
Date August 2, 1992

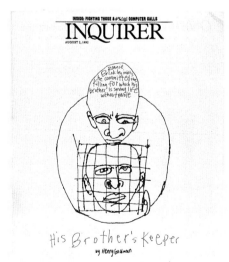

Publication The Washington Post Magazine
Award Merit
Art Director Kelly Doe
Designer Kelly Doe
Illustrator David Hughes
Publisher The Washington Post Co.
Category Illustration/Single Page or Spread
Date July 26, 1992

Publication The Washington Post Magazine
Award Merit
Art Director Richard Baker
Designer Kelly Doe
Illustrator Janet Woolley
Publisher The Washington Post Co.
Category Illustration/Single Page or Spread
Date November 1, 1992

Publication	Details
Award	Gold
Art Director	B.W. Honeycutt
Designers	B.W Honeycutt, Markus Kiersztan
Illustrators	Peter Bagge, Jonathon Rosen,
	Gilberto Hernandez, Kaz,
	Bob Camp, Mack White,
	Dan Cowles, Drew Friedman,
	Ivan Velez, Jr., Maurice Vellekoop,
	Dean Rohrer,
	Kyle Baker
Publisher	Condé Nast Publishing Co., Inc.
Category	Illustration/Story
Date	August 1992

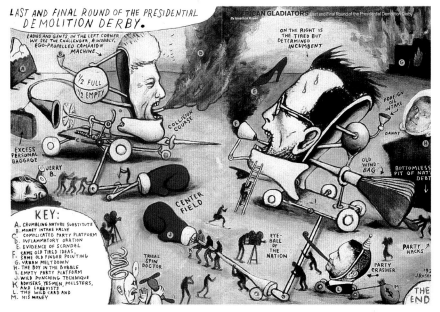

Publication	The New York Times Magazine
Award	Silver
Art Director	Janet Froelich
Designer	Kandy Littrell
Illustrator	Ross MacDonald
Publisher	The New York Times
Category	Illustration/Story
Date	February 16, 1992

The New York Times Magazine

FEBRUARY 16, 1992 / SECTION 6

50 YEARS OF

Crossword Puzzles

A
SPECIAL
SECTION
PAGE 29

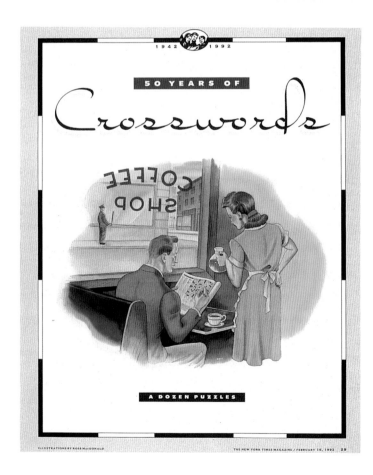

1942 — 1992

50 YEARS OF

Crosswords

COFFEE SHOP

A DOZEN PUZZLES

ILLUSTRATIONS BY ROSS MacDONALD / THE NEW YORK TIMES MAGAZINE / FEBRUARY 16, 1992   29

Diarist Anaïs? Why, Pin, of course — and mourn for the mangled words strewn about. But on the other hand there was something deeply satisfying in the knowledge that errors as much as truths could be made to fit in the pattern. Everything has its place in a puzzle, and the place is communal. Solving means weaving the ups through the downs, the animals through the minerals, the obscure actresses through the dictators and czars until the whole world's trivia have been turned into a tapestry.

I wanted in. A family of economists in the neighborhood had bought a copier solely to solve the Sunday puzzle problem; the best we could do in my house was persuade my father to work his magic in pencil. That way, at least, I could come along later, busy myself cleaning the untidy room of his first attempts — change "Pin" to "Nin" as neces-

BY ANNE FOX   EDITED BY WILL WENG

GREETINGS À LA BERLITZ

DEC. 23, 1973: A challenging example of using interlocking long entries, made even more difficult because of the limitations of the subject. Answers on page 50.

ACROSS
1 Queens battleground
5 Ex-frosh
9 —— and Kashmir
14 Sky Way
19 Famous also-rans
20 African plant
21 Sky Hunter
22 Papal cape
23 Hebrew measure
24 Festive
25 —— juste
26 Star in 21 Across
27 Words from a Spanish carol
31 Roman official
32 "—— prayer for me"
33 Kafka character
34 Old Roman province
35 N. L. player
37 Southern constellation
40 Hitting stats
43 A Roosevelt
45 Recoverable sea goods
47 Burdened
49 Words by Isaac Watts
55 Like a 10-cent tip
56 Bridge work
57 Having a handle
58 Suffix with boy or girl
59 Dance
60 This: Sp.
61 Words from a French carol
71 Nightingale trademark
72 Female sprite
73 Cereal grass
74 Craving
77 Lay low
89 Sensitive plant
83 Words from a German carol
86 Cleaving tools
87 Duvalier land
88 Do C.P.A. work
89 Tree
90 Some prizes
91 Red or Charing
94 —— Ferry
98 One of the Joneses
101 Silvers
102 Outdoor stairway
103 Words from an Italian carol
110 Lamblike
111 Korean city
112 Willing

113 One's own: Prefix
114 Large bill
115 Miss Bryant
116 Roman date
117 Medical Nobelist, 1970
119 Absolute
120 Parts
120 Gotham postal initials
121 Arizona town

DOWN
1 Pushed
2 Honshu port
3 Of deserts
4 Stony meteorites
5 Long tales
6 Norwegian saint
7 May fixture
8 San Simeon name
9 U.S. carol
10 Place of action
11 Opera role
12 Word with light or shine
13 "Render therefore ——"
14 Principled
15 Irritating
16 Little Flower
17 Swiss painter
18 Tiger, e.g.

28 Marine conger
29 Swiss river
30 Pasture sound
35 Speech part: Abbr.
36 Sentence structure
37 Arab head cord
38 Grade
39 Wildebeest
41 Penchant
42 Dean of St. Paul's
44 U.S. author
46 Kind of hill
47 Slow, in music
48 Indian state
49 French girl friend
50 Hencoop feature
51 Actress Arlene
52 "To ——!"
53 Pisgah summit
54 Slight taste
60 English river
62 Equally
63 Juliet's betrothed
64 Sobeit
65 S.A. monkey
66 Battle and pole
67 Utah mountains
68 Heath

69 Let up
70 The Man
74 Face
75 Green land
76 Winner pileup
77 To-do
78 Floral greetings
79 River isle
80 Pre-

81 In the same place: Lat.
82 Vehicle
84 Roderick
85 Edwards of vaudeville days
90 Charlene
92 Tease
93 Alkene

95 Type of veil
96 Food fish
97 Ready for sleep
99 Mother of Lavinia
100 Plastic for flooring
101 Shoshonean: Var.

102 Garden plant
103 Adroit
104 Hodgepodge
105 Eskers
106 Certain divorce
107 Drudgery
108 Astor or Jane Grey
109 Très ——

ILLUSTRATIONS BY ROSS MacDONALD   THE NEW YORK TIMES MAGAZINE / FEBRUARY 16, 1992   43

Publication Condé Nast Traveler
Award Merit
Design Director Diana LaGuardia
Art Director Christin Gangi
Designer Audrey Razgaitis
Illustrator Barry Blitt
Publisher Condé Nast Publishing Co., Inc.
Category Illustration/Story
Date November 1992

Traveler's life

The great american wine trail

YOU CAN TASTE THE PLACE WHEN you drink a good wine—taste the territory that nourished the wine, taste the essential character of the region. In that sense, wine is its own guide to place. And as America produces more and more world-class wines, so American vineyards are becoming part of the travel experience. To sample the very best American wines, we called in a panel of experts. They blind-tasted 225 recent vintages from ten states. On the following pages, our wine correspondent JOSEPH WARD assesses the winners and we highlight three West Coast wine regions with tours of their vineyards.

ILLUSTRATIONS BY BARRY BLITT

Publication The Atlantic Monthly
Award Merit
Design Director Judy Garlan
Art Director Judy Garlan
Designer Judy Garlan
Illustrator David Pohl
Publisher The Atlantic Monthly
Category Illustration/Story
Date October 1992

Publication	Discover
Award	Merit
Art Director	David Armario
Designer	James Lambertus
Illustrator	Jonathon Rosen
Publisher	Disney Magazine Publishing
Category	Illustration/Story
Date	December 1992

GENETIC SURPRISES

BY JEROLD M. LOWENSTEIN

SOME SERIOUSLY WEIRD
THINGS ARE SPRINGING
OUT OF THE TWISTED
TANGLE OF OUR DNA.

ILLUSTRATIONS BY JONATHAN ROSEN

Myotonic dystrophy is a degenerative muscle disorder whose victims can grip but can't let go. They may also suffer from such bewildering and seemingly disparate symptoms as cataracts, abnormal

IT WAS BAD ENOUGH TO FIND GENES INHABITED BY INTRONS.
BUT GENES INSIDE INTRONS INHABITING GENES, LIKE SO
MANY CHINESE BOXES, WAS SOMETHING ELSE AGAIN

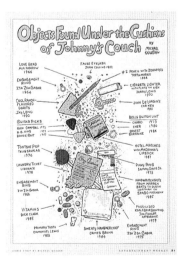

Publication	Entertainment Weekly
Award	Merit
Design Director	Michael Grossman
Art Director	Mark Michaelson
Designer	Elizabeth Betts
Illustrators	Linda Barry, Mark Zingarelli, Michael Dougan, Drew Friedman, Ben Katchor, Mark Alan Stamaty
Publisher	Entertainment Weekly, Inc.
Category	Illustration/Story
Date	May 9, 1992

Publication	Entertainment Weekly
Award	Merit
Design Director	Michael Grossman
Art Director	Mark Michaelson
Designer	Michael Grossman
Illustrators	Josh Gosfield, Nola Lopez
Publisher	Entertainment Weekly, Inc.
Category	Illustration/Story
Date	December 25, 1992

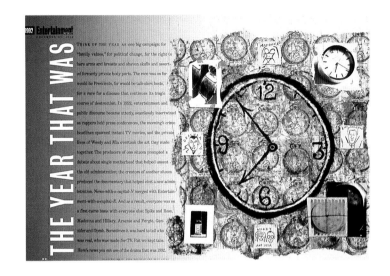

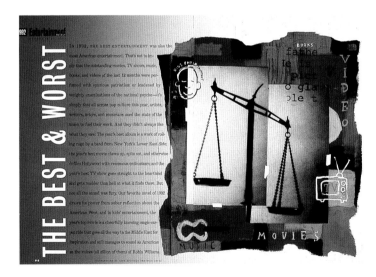

Publication Health
Award Merit
Art Director Jane Palecek
Designer Jane Palecek
Illustrators Anita Kunz, Josh Gosfield, Matt Mahurin
Photographer Nola Lopez
Publisher Health
Category Illustration/Story
Date January 1992

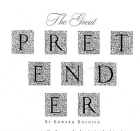

The Great
PRET END ER

BY EDWARD DOLNICK

LIKE SO MANY peculiarly matched pairs in the big city, we met

Illustration by Anita Kunz

SHE WAS THE MOST AMAZING WOMAN I'D EVER MET, FULL OF ANECDOTES ABOUT HER CALAMITOUS LIFE AND HER RICH FRIENDS. THEN SHE SAID THAT SHE WAS A PATHOLOGICAL LIAR. WHAT WAS I TO BELIEVE?

One man, posing as an astronaut, showed his wife kitchen tiles and said they fell off the Challenger shuttle. "I loved the man I thought I was married to," she said.

My task was to play detective in a house of mirrors. I had to know whether her "true" stories were true, but also whether she was really lying about the lies.

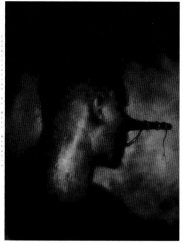

TALES
WITH A BOO

What are you scared of?
They're only campfire chillers...

ILLUSTRATIONS BY BLAIR DRAWSON

THE
BONFIRE

By Valerie Frankel

STOP THE
SCREAMS

By Marilyn Johnson

TASTE OF
THE KILL

By Donovan Webster

FLAMES
OF DESIRE

By Craig Vetter

Publication Outside
Award Merit
Design Director John Askwith
Art Directors Pat Prather, Paula Kreiter Turelli
Designer Dave Allen
Illustrator Blair Drawson
Publisher Mariah Publications
Category Illustration/Story
Date August 1992

Publication Psychology Today
Award Merit
Design Director Robert J. George
Illustrator Jordin Isip
Publisher Sussex Publishers
Category Illustration/Story
Date September/October 1992

HOW A LEGACY OF
CHILD ABUSE LEADS
TO HOMICIDE • BY
KATHLEEN M. HEIDE

WHY
KIDS
KILL PARENTS

**The killing is an act of desperation—
the only way out of a family situation of
abuse they can no longer endure.**

**The true killer is child mistreatment.
The carnage includes the death of the
human spirit from persistent abuse.**

Publication Special Report
Award Merit
Design Director Doug Renfro
Designer Pamela S. Smith
Illustrators Sandra Hendler, Laura Levine, Mary Anne Lloyd,
Gary Baseman, Anita Kunz, Guy Billout, Peter Johnson,
Alan E. Cober, John Hersey, Stéphan Daigle, Lane Smith,
Randall Enos, Gene Greif, Josh Goshfield, Julian Allen
Publisher Whittle Communications
Category Illustration/Story
Date February/April 1992

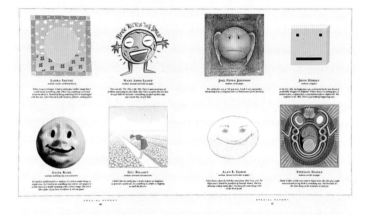

The Painted Island

Publication Travel Holiday
Award Merit
Design Director Teresa Fernandes
Designer Lou DiLorenzo
Illustrators Julian Allen
Publisher Readers Digest Publications
Category Illustration/Story
Date June 1992

Publication Wordperfect Magazine
Award Merit
Art Director Ron Stucki
Designer Don Lambson
Illustrator Chris Gall
Publisher Wordperfect Publishing
Category Illustration/Story
Date January 1992

175

476

Publication	Bloomberg Magazine
Award	Merit
Art Director	Sarah Stearns
Illustrator	C.F. Payne
Publisher	Michael Bloomberg
Category	Illustration/Story
Date	September 1992

568

Publication	Frankfurter Allgemeine Magazin
Award	Merit
Design Director	Hans-Georg Pospischil
Illustrator	Seymour Chwast
Publisher	Frankfurter Allgemeine Magazin
Studio	The Pushpin Group, Inc.
Category	Illustration/Story
Date	March 6, 1992

The Sprucey Pond

We ice-skated and decorated the bottom tree while listening to Charles Dickens's classic story about Tiny Tim dramatized on the Victrola, or Tchaikovsky's "Nutcracker Suite," or to Bing Crosby singing "Silent Night" in his wonderful, whisky, shower-stall voice.

M aybe the best of Christmas for me meant black ice on Taggart's Pond, two miles away, with enough of a wind to blow the new dusting of snow off the surface, but not so much that we were chilled. Twelve was a kind of magical age (I've had some others: 21, 30, 44, 55 . . .), and after my parents and little sister and I had skated for a while, I'd finally straddle our setter-dog, Flush, on my two blades, cling his eager shoulders and let him pull me as he raced the length of the pond, remembering to let go before he bounded into the rocks and spruce trees ashore—then call him back for a replay, and he got as tired as I.

In the summer, Flush and I explored Taggart's Pond in search of four-foot water snakes and three-foot snapping turtles, but my father would be on the golf course, my mother at her garden club, my sister (at a later age) learning to ride a horse, and so the whole point about Christmas was that for once we came together   *(Continued on page 89)*

Edward Hoagland is the author, most recently, of "Balancing Acts," a collection of essays. He is at work as a novelist.

By Edward Hoagland

ILLUSTRATION BY ROSS MACDONALD

"Sometimes in life you just got to stop runnin'." Pouting, tight-lipped, nodding, taken with his own words, both cops staring at him, the room quiet now for "It's a Wonderful Life" walking in from Ann's Thrift down the hall, "You just got to stop runnin'," Mo repeated, loving the sound of it, the drama.

The Plea

C hump Carroll wouldn't have busted Mo James at all, especially on the night before Christmas, except for the way Mo had gone about the whole situation. First of all, when he was selling in *in front of the Gary Motel* right off Route 3, stopping the customers before they could drive up and around to the rear where the action was supposed to be, where Chump and his partner, Curry, could trap them, cause grief, keep things under control. Second, he didn't belong to the motel crowd. He was an outsider and his hustling out there was unfair to the regular lowlifes whom Chump and Curry had a sense of family with. Third, when Chump spotted him working the front he waved the dope at the high, cone-shitted weeds alongside the highway by the road McDonald's wrappers and beer cans for an hour or order to come up with only two pathetic $10 bottles of coke. And last of all, worst of all, he ran.

So now Mo James, 64, 130 pounds in heaven pants, white T-shirt and a Triple P.A.T. Gator pants chopped by the elbows, sat in the overheated, fluorescently lit detectives' room above the motor vehicle bureau and the Town Court, his hands cuffed   *(Continued on page 89)*

Richard Price, a novelist and screenwriter, is author of "Clockers."

By Richard Price

ILLUSTRATION BY GARY BASEMAN

It may be that she and Bonnie do not present the spectacle of gray exhaustion and bleak rage that Mary Ann thinks they do, but most of their fellow shoppers are smiling, and some are beaming along with the piped-in Christmas carols. The bags and packages they are carrying look promising and richly heavy. The groups of teen-age girls who always roam the mall today look almost innocent.

A Quarrelsome Peace

T he reason Mary Ann makes her first mistake is that Bonnie's anguished cry, as she throws herself down in front of the Christmas tree, happens to stape her from one of these nonsafar sleeps she can achieve only in the afternoon. Of course Mary Ann jerks upward in a panic. Of course she doesn't know where she is, only that Bonnie needs something. Of course, when Bonnie screeches, "We haven't bought a present for Mr. Jones," Mary Ann tries to employ her calmest, most conciliatory manner. She barely realizes what she is saying — this is the mistake. "We can go to the mall now, if you like."

Bonnie rises from the carpet immediately and goes to the closet for her coat. It takes Mary Ann considerably longer to rise from the couch, because she is now nicely pregnant (due after New Year's), and despite the conversation she is still merely comatose.

She moves in a heavy daze toward her coat and her purse. She

Jane Smiley's most recent novel is "A Thousand Acres," for which she won the 1992 Pulitzer Prize.

By Jane Smiley

ILLUSTRATION BY ANTHONY RUSSO

Publication The New York Times Magazine
Award Merit
Art Director Janet Froelich
Designers Kathi Rota, Kandy Littrell
Illustrators John Collier, David Sandlin, Ross MacDonald
Publisher The New York Times
Category Illustration/Story
Date December 28, 1992

Publication LA Style
Award Merit
Design Director Lloyd Ziff
Designers Lloyd Ziff, Walter Schoenauer
Illustrator Malcolm Tarlofsky
Publisher American Express Publishing
Category Illustration/Story
Date June 1992

A PASSAGE TO SENSUALITY

One couple's lesson in the art of tantric sex

We should expand our sexuality to include a soft-on.

PHOTOGRAPHY

Still Life

single page or spread

Fashion

STORY

Travel

Beauty

PHOTOJOURNALISM

Portraits

interiors

TRAVEL

Detail from
photograph by
Jack Dykinga for
Outside

Publication	Parenting
Award	Gold
Art Director	Dian Aziza - Ooka
Designer	Allyson Appen
Photographer	Robert Holmgren
Photo Editor	Tripp Mikich
Category	Photography/Photojournalism, Portraits
Date	October 1992

ARE YOU DAD ENOUGH?

BY PENELOPE LEACH

Publication Rolling Stone
Award Silver
Art Director Fred Woodward
Designer Angela Skouras
Photographer Albert Watson
Photo Editor Laurie Kratochvil
Publisher Straight Arrow Publishers, Inc.
Category Photography/Photojournalism, Portraits
Date October 29, 1992

Publication Rolling Stone
Award Silver
Art Director Fred Woodward
Designer Fred Woodward
Photographer Albert Watson
Photo Editor Laurie Kratochvil
Publisher Straight Arrow Publishers, Inc.
Category Photography/Photojournalism, Portraits
Date February 6, 1992

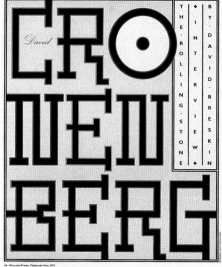

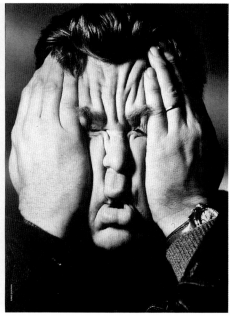

John Goodman Is Some Babe

Who better to play Babe Ruth than big John Goodman, a complicated guy with a large appetite and an even larger talent

By Peter Richmond

A silver-blue midtown-Manhattan December dusk, the time of day at the time of year when the city is alight with something more than Christmas windows and the whole town is buoyed with a singular exuberance in spite of itself—on this day, no one more so than John Goodman, in old jeans and a brown leather jacket worn into submission, sitting at the bar in a well-lit place off Central Park South, trading bourbon with beer while he grabs big chunks of America off the shelves.

"Look at what Perkins did for Fitzgerald!"—a small sip of the bourbon, a big swallow of the

Publication GQ
Award Silver
Creative Director Robert Priest
Designer Robert Priest
Photographer Gregory Heisler
Photo Editor Karen Frank
Publisher Condé Nast Publications
Category Photography/Photojournalism, Portraits
Date April 1992

Publication	Details
Award	Merit
Art Director	B.W. Honeycutt
Designer	Brian Kobberger
Photographer	Ellen von Unwerth
Photo Editor	Greg Pond
Publisher	Condé Nast Publishing Co., Inc.
Category	Photography/Photojournalism, Portraits
Date	December 1992

Publication	Details
Award	Merit
Art Director	B.W. Honeycutt
Photographer	Albert Watson
Photo Editor	Greg Pond
Publisher	Condé Nast Publishing Co., Inc.
Category	Photography/Photojournalism, Portraits
Date	January 1992

music

Sade

With the release of her new LP, *Love deluxe*, the queen of romance comes clean about kissing, kickboxing, and her sweetest taboo: love and marriage

"Gary's coffin for *Dracula* has arrived. "You're going to sleep in it, aren't you?" He laughs. "You think I'm sick?"

music

John Lydon

Having a Rotten time with the man from Public Image Ltd.
By Tom Hibbert

alzheimer's stepchild

A NEUROPATHOLOGIST defies conventional wisdom when he swears there's a connection between aluminum and Alzheimer's.

BY PETER RADETSKY

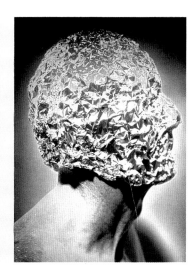

Publication	Details
Award	Merit
Art Director	B.W. Honeycutt
Designer	Laura Genninger
Photographer	Juergen Teller
Photo Editor	Greg Pond
Publisher	Condé Nast Publishing Co., Inc.
Category	Photography/Photojournalism, Portraits
Date	March 1992

Publication	Discover
Award	Merit
Art Director	David Armario
Designers	David Armario, James Lambertus
Photographer	Geof Kern
Publisher	Disney Magazine Publishing
Category	Photography/Photojournalism, Portraits
Date	September 1992

Publication Entertainment Weekly
Award Merit
Design Director Michael Grossman
Art Director Mark Michaelson
Designer Mark Michaelson
Photographer Silvia Otte
Photo Editors Mary Dunn, Doris Brautigan
Publisher Entertainment Weekly, Inc.
Category Photography/Photojournalism, Portraits
Date May 1, 1992

Publication Entertainment Weekly
Award Merit
Design Director Michael Grossman
Art Director Mark Michaelson
Designer Mark Michaelson
Photographer Chris Buck
Photo Editors Mary Dunn, Michelle Romero
Publisher Entertainment Weekly, Inc.
Category Photography/Photojournalism, Portraits
Date October 16, 1992

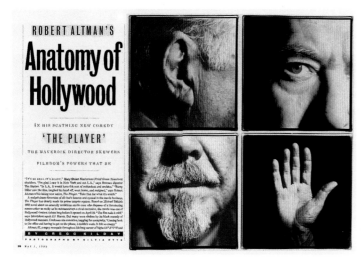

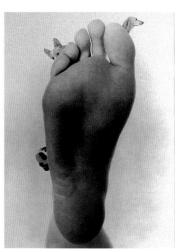

Publication GQ
Award Merit
Creative Director Robert Priest
Designer Robert Priest
Photographer Brian Smale
Photo Editor Karen Frank
Publisher Condé Nast Publications
Category Photography/Photojournalism, Portraits
Date September 1992

Publication Health
Award Merit
Art Director Jane Palecek
Designer Dorothy Marschall
Photographer Geof Kern
Publisher Health
Category Photography/Photojournalism, Portraits
Date November/December 1992

Publication House and Garden Magazine (HG)
Award Merit
Design Director Dania Martinez-Davey
Photographer Irving Penn
Photo Editor Susan Goldberger
Publisher Condé Nast Publishing Co., Inc.
Category Photography/Photojournalism, Portraits
Date October 1992

Publication Men's Journal
Award Merit
Art Director Matthew Drace
Designer Matthew Drace
Photographer Len Irish
Publisher Straight Arrow Publishers
Category Photography/Photojournalism, Portraits
Date November/December 1992

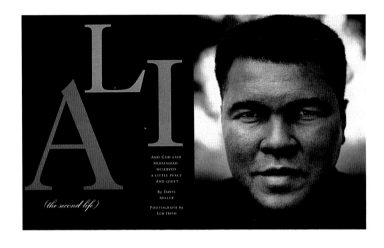

Publication Rolling Stone
Award Merit
Art Director Fred Woodward
Designer Debra Bishop
Photographer Albert Watson
Photo Editor Laurie Kratochvil
Publisher Straight Arrow Publishers
Category Photography/Photojournalism, Portraits
Date October 29, 1992

Publication Self
Award Merit
Design Directors Beatrice Muñoz, Yolanda Cuomo
Designer Beatrice Muñoz
Photographer Donna Ferrato
Photo Editor Leslie Goodman
Publisher Condé Nast Publishing Co., Inc.
Category Photography/Photojournalism, Portraits
Date December 1992

Publication	Special Report
Award	Merit
Design Director	Doug Renfro
Designer	Andrea De Bevoise
Photographer	Mary Ellen Mark
Photo Editor	Kathy Getsey
Publisher	Whittle Communications
Category	Photography/Photojournalism, Portraits
Date	November 1991/January 1992

Publication	Spin
Award	Merit
Art Director	Stephen Webster
Designer	Elizabeth Grubaugh
Photographer	Anton Corbijn
Photo Editor	Shana Sobel
Publisher	Camouflage Associates
Category	Photography/Photojournalism, Portraits
Date	February 1992

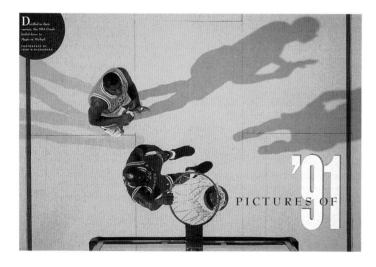

Publication	Sports Illustrated
Award	Merit
Design Director	Steven Hoffman
Designer	Ed Truscio
Photographer	John W. McDonough
Photo Editor	Karen Mullarkey
Publisher	Time Inc. Magazine Company
Category	Photography/Photojournalism, Portraits
Date	December 1991/January 1992

Publication	Sports Illustrated
Award	Merit
Design Director	Steven Hoffman
Art Director	F. Darrin Perry
Designer	F. Darrin Perry
Photographer	Walter Iooss, Jr.
Photo Editor	Heinz Kluetmeier
Publisher	Time Inc. Magazine Company
Category	Photography/Photojournalism, Portraits
Date	July 22, 1992

Publication	Us
Award	Merit
Art Director	Pamela Berry
Designer	Sarika Aggarwal
Photographer	Glen Erler
Publisher	Straight Arrow Publishers
Category	Photography/Photojournalism, Portraits
Date	August 1992

Publication	Art & Auction
Award	Merit
Art Director	David O'Connor
Designer	David O'Connor
Photographer	McDermott & McGough
Publisher	Art & Auction Joint Ventures
Category	Photography/Photojournalism, Portraits
Date	May 1992

Publication	Graphis
Award	Merit
Design Director	B. Martin Pedersen
Art Director	B. Martin Pedersen
Designer	B. Martin Pedersen
Photographer	Hiro
Publisher	Graphis US, Inc.
Category	Photography/Photojournalism, Portraits
Date	March/April 1992

Publication	Graphis
Award	Merit
Design Director	B. Martin Pedersen
Art Directors	B. Martin Pedersen, Randell Pearson
Designer	B. Martin Pedersen
Photographer	Arnold Neuman
Publisher	Graphis US, Inc.
Category	Photography/Photojournalism, Portraits
Date	January/February 1992

Publication Graphis
Award Merit
Design Director B. Martin Pedersen
Art Director B. Martin Pedersen
Designer B. Martin Pedersen
Photographer Michelle Clement
Publisher Graphis US, Inc.
Category Photography/Photojournalism, Portraits
Date January/February 1992

Publication Macworld
Award Merit
Design Director Dennis M cLeod
Art Director Joanne Hoffman
Designer Tim Johnson
Photographer Brian Smale
Publisher Macworld Communications
Category Photography/Photojournalism, Portraits
Date January 1992

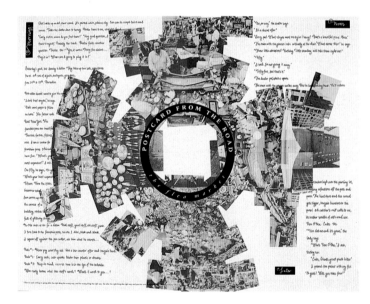

Publication Value Newsletter
Award Merit
Design Director Ken Cook
Designer Kathleen Dolan
Photographer David McGlynn
Studio Ken Cook Design
Client Hopper Paper
Category Photography/Photojournalism, Portraits
Date Fall 1992

Publication World
Award Merit
Art Director Donna Bonavita
Designer Donna Bonavita
Photographer John Isaac
Publisher KPMG Peat Marwick, Communications Group
Category Photography/Photojournalism, Portraits
Date May 1992

Publication Corrections Corporation of America Annual Report
Award Merit
Art Directors Jan Elis, Laurie Ellis
Designers Jan Elis, Laurie Ellis
Photographer Mark Tucker
Studio Ellis Design
Client Corrections Corporation
Category Photography/Photojournalism, Portraits
Date 1992

Publication The New York Times/Arts & Leisure
Award Merit
Art Director Linda Brewer
Designer Linda Brewer
Photographer David McGlynn
Publisher The New York Times
Category Photography/Photojournalism, Portraits
Date June 21, 1992

Publication The New York Times Magazine
Award Merit
Art Director Janet Froelich
Photographer Michael O'Brien
Photo Editor Kathy Ryan
Publisher The New York Times
Category Photography/Photojournalism, Portraits
Date January 19, 1992

Publication The New York Times Magazine
Award Merit
Art Director Janet Froelich
Designer Charlene Benson
Photographer Silvia Otte
Photo Editor Kathy Ryan
Publisher The New York Times
Category Photography/Photojournalism, Portraits
Date September 13, 1992

Publication The New York Times Magazine
Award Merit
Art Director Janet Froelich
Designer Kathi Rota
Photographer William Wegman
Photo Editor Kathy Ryan
Publisher The New York Times
Category Photography/Photojournalism, Portraits
Date May 17, 1992

Publication The New York Times Magazine
Award Merit
Art Director Janet Froelich
Photographer Nigel Parry
Photo Editor Kathy Ryan
Publisher The New York Times
Category Photography/Photojournalism, Portraits
Date April 5, 1992

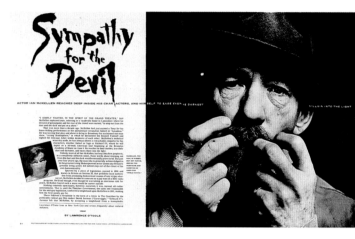

Publication The New York Times Magazine
Award Merit
Art Director Janet Froelich
Designer Kathy Rota
Photographer Dan Winters
Photo Editor Kathy Ryan
Publisher The New York Times
Category Photography/Photojournalism, Portraits
Date October 25, 1992

Publication The New York Times Magazine
Award Merit
Art Director Janet Froelich
Designer Janet Froelich
Photographer Chester Higgins Jr.
Photo Editor Kathy Ryan
Publisher The New York Times
Category Photography/Photojournalism, Portraits
Date April 19, 1992

Publication The New York Times Magazine
Award Merit
Art Director Janet Froelich
Designer Kandy Littrell
Photographer Andrew Eccles
Photo Editor Kathy Ryan
Publisher The New York Times
Category Photography/Photojournalism, Portraits
Date May 31, 1992

Publication The New York Times Magazine
Award Merit
Art Director Janet Froelich
Designer Kathi Rota
Photographer Danielle Weil
Photo Editor Kathy Ryan
Publisher The New York Times
Category Photography/Photojournalism, Portraits
Date March 8, 1992

Publication The New York Times Magazine
Award Merit
Art Director Janet Froelich
Designer Kandy Littrell
Photographer Jon Jones
Photo Editor Kathy Ryan
Publisher The New York Times
Category Photography/Photojournalism,
Portraits
Date July 26, 1992

Publication The New York Times Magazine
Award Merit
Art Director Janet Froelich
Designer Kandy Littrell
Photographer Sally Mann
Photo Editor Kathy Ryan
Publisher The New York Times
Category Photography/Photojournalism, Portraits
Date September 27, 1992

Publication The New York Times Magazine
Award Merit
Art Director Janet Froelich
Designer Kandy Littrell
Photographer Marc Asnin
Photo Editor Kathy Ryan
Publisher The New York Times
Category Photography/Photojournalism,
Portraits
Date March 15, 1992

Publication Vogue
Award Silver
Art Director Raul Martinez
Designer Eric Pryor
Photographer Raymond Meier
Photo Editor Esin Goknar
Publisher Condé Nast Publishing Co., Inc.
Category Photography/Still Life, Interiors, Travel
Date August 1992

simply red

No mere condiment, ketchup is a culinary triumph, America's greatest sauce. But which ketchup? In his search for the ideal, Jeffrey Steingarten ransacks history and samples nearly 57 varieties

In England there are sixty different religions, and only one sauce.
—Marquis Domenico Caracciolo (1715–1789)

When rumor recently reached my ears that U.S. sales of salsa would soon eclipse those of ketchup, catsup, and catchup (these words are synonyms), I rushed down to my local supermarket, planted myself in the ketchup department, and stood a lonely, anxious vigil, as though my plump presence alone could staunch the tide of chunky, piquant salsa that menaced from the opposite end of Aisle 5.

I yield to no one in my toleration of multiculturalism in America. I eagerly celebrate Cinco de Mayo, Chinese New Year, the festa of San Gennaro, and the decay of the Ottoman Empire with whatever banquet is most fitting. But ketchup's fall to second-class status is another thing entirely. And that is what the packaged-food experts predict. According to *Fortune*, sales of "Mexican sauces" will reach $802 million in 1992, leaving ketchup in the dust at $723. Even worse, the gap will widen for three more years.

To my mind, ketchup stands in the top tier of the world's cold or tepid nondessert sauces. It is surely our proudest, perhaps our only, homegrown sauce achievement. Marquis Domenico Caracciolo, ambassador from Naples to England, was probably referring to *crème anglaise*, the greatest dessert sauce ever created, but he might as well have been talking ketchup. Ninety-seven percent of American homes keep ketchup in the kitchen. Each of us blissfully eats three bottles of it a year. A tablespoon of ketchup is packed with flavor but carries only sixteen calories and no fat; it is recommended for dieters and skinny people alike. Pour tablespoons of ketchup, the amount you might consume on a hamburger and a large order of fries, are the nutritional equivalent of an entire ripe medium tomato, with none of the fuss and bother.

Ketchup is "one of the great successes the sauce world has ever known," wrote Elisabeth Rozin in *The Journal of Gastronomy* (Summer, 1988). In its brilliant red color, its rich flavor, and its marked salinity, Rozin theorizes, ketchup represents the "fulfillment, both real and symbolic, of the ancient and atavistic lust for blood," magically achieved with the use of plant products alone. Rozin also draws an analogy to the Christian Mass and its fruity surrogate for the blood of Christ, but I forget how it goes. All I know is that I discovered a case of Del Monte in one of the celebrated kitchens of Piemonte, in northern Italy, vying with *tartufi*

and *porcini* for the chef's affections. And last year in Paris, in a kitchen soon to receive its second Michelin star, I watched the chef add a dollop of Heinz to his sauce of salmon's blood, red wine, and *verjus*, a postmodernization of Escoffier's sauce *genevoise*. Miguel de Cervantes once wrote, "La mejor salsa del mundo es la hambre"—the best sauce in the world is the hunger. Cervantes had obviously never tasted ketchup.

Will 1992 be the year that we abandon our own great sauce, our most-excellent ketchup?

Briefly leaving my shopping cart on guard, I bought a bag of potato chips (natural flavor, not rancho or nacho) and a plastic squeeze bottle of Heinz ketchup, the standard by which all other ketchups, for better or worse, must be measured. I swirled some Heinz on a potato chip and munched thoughtfully.

Before long, my mood had brightened. The article in *Fortune* was surely a false alarm; either the magazine does not know its sauces, or else it has deliberately set out to undermine America's confidence in its own condiments. Comparing the sales of all Mexican sauces to the sales of ketchup, just one sauce, is unjust and misleading. Just think of the multitude of sauces in Mexican cuisine, their *mole de olla* and *mole verde de pepita*, red *sesame* seed sauce and green tomato sauce, *salsa borracha* and *salsa de los reyes*, *salsa de moscas* and *salsa de ajero*, chili sauces made with *pasillas* and with *cascabels*, with *chiles de árbol* and *chiles de guajillo*! When sales of *mole verde de pepita* exceed those of Heinz, then we will have something to worry about.

I edged warily down the aisle to the shelves of salsa. A glance at the unit-pricing stickers under each brand again proved that ketchup still reigns supreme. The average price for a quart of ketchup in my supermarket came to $1.16; the salsas averaged $5.50. Divide the first price into the second and you'll see that on whatever day in 1992 dollar sales of all the salsas put together exceed those of ketchup, ketchup will still be 4.74 times more popular than salsa because salsa is 4.74 times more expensive.

I left the supermarket in a gay and celebratory mood and in possession of every type of ketchup they had on offer, nine in all. Within a few days I had ransacked the other markets in my ▶ 298

Photographer: Raymond Meier

244

Publication	American Health
Award	Merit
Art Director	Mark Danzig
Designer	Susan Gockel Dazzo
Photographers	Bradford Walker , Evans Hitz
Photo Editor	Kate Sullivan
Publisher	Readers Digest Publications
Category	Photography/Still Life, Interiors, Travel
Date	January/February 1992

Publication	American Health
Award	Merit
Art Director	Mark Danzig
Designer	Mark Danzig
Photographer	Michael Llewellyn
Photo Editor	Kate Sullivan
Publisher	Readers Digest Publications
Category	Photography/Still Life, Interiors, Travel
Date	June 1992

Publication	American Health
Award	Merit
Art Director	Mark Danzig
Designers	Susan Gockel, Dazzo
Photographer	Kenneth Willardt
Photo Editor	Kate Sullivan
Publisher	Readers Digest Publications
Category	Photography/Still Life, Interiors, Travel
Date	July/August 1992

Publication	European Travel & Life
Award	Merit
Art Director	Jeanne Dzienciol
Designer	Jeanne Dzienciol
Photographer	Robert Rattner
Publisher	K-III Magazines
Category	Photography/Still Life, Interiors, Travel
Date	February 1992

Publication House Beautiful
Award Merit
Art Director Andrzej Janerka
Designer Andrzej Janerka
Photographer Yoan
Publisher The Hearst Corporation
Category Photography/Still Life, Interiors, Travel
Date October 1992

Publication GQ
Award Merit
Design Director Robert Priest
Designer Robert Priest
Photographer Hiro
Photo Editor Karen Frank
Publisher Condé Nast Publications
Category Photography/Still Life, Interiors, Travel
Date May 1992

IN THE GARDEN

The subject is rose books

Rose species number more than 2,000. But don't despair. New guides tell which are easy to grow

Of Mollusks And Men

Forget sex. To ingest the slimy and possibly toxic oyster is to ratify everything else we Americans hold dear

By Tom Junod

Balancing the Books

Publication Macworld
Award Merit
Design Director Dennis McLeod
Art Director Joanne Hoffman
Designer Tim Johnson
Photographer Hugh Kretschmer
Publisher Macworld Communications
Category Photography/Still Life, Interiors, Travel
Date November 1992

Publication Travel Holiday
Award Merit
Art Director Lou Di Lorenzo
Designer Lou Di Lorenzo
Photographer Dennis Marsico
Photo Editor Bill Black
Publisher Readers Digest Publications
Studio Travel Holiday
Category Photography/Still Life, Interiors, Travel
Date November 1992

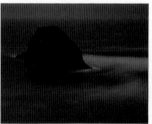

Publication Outside
Award Merit
Design Director John Askwith
Art Directors Pat Prather, Paula Kreiter Turelli
Designer Dave Allen
Photographers Jack Dykinga, Tim Crosby
Photo Editor Larry Ev ans
Publisher Mariah Publications Corporation
Category Photography/Still Life, Interiors, Travel
Date November 1992

Publication The Washington Post Magazine
Award Merit
Art Director Richard Baker
Designer Richard Baker
Photographers Stuart Waston, Alan Richardson
Photo Editor Karen Tanaka
Publisher The Washington Post Co.
Category Photography/Still Life, Interiors, Travel
Date March 29, 1992

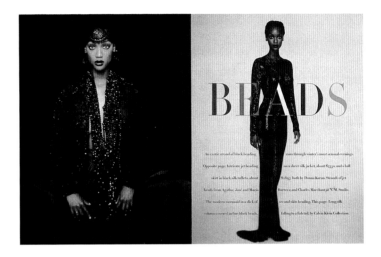

Publication Harper's Bazaar
Award Merit
Creative Director Fabien Baron
Art Director Joel Berg
Designer Johan Svensson
Photographer Paolo Roversi
Publisher The Hearst Corporation
Category Photography/ Fashion, Beauty
Date November 1992

Publication The New York Times Magazine
Award Merit
Art Director Janet Froelich
Designer Kandy Littrell
Photographer Sally Gall
Photo Editor Kathy Ryan
Publisher The New York Times
Category Photography/Still Life, Interiors, Travel
Date June 7, 1992

Publication The New York Times Magazine
Award Gold
Art Director Janet Froelich
Designer Janet Froelich
Photographer James Nachtwey
Photo Editor Kathy Ryan
Publisher The New York Times
Category Photography Story/
Photojournalism, Portraits
Date December 6, 1992

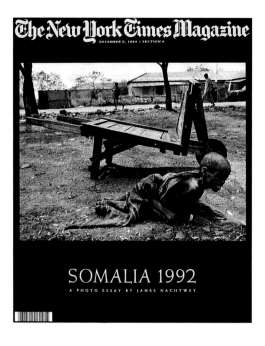

Publication The New York Times Magazine
Award Gold
Art Director Janet Froelich
Designer Kathi Rota
Photographer Sebastiao Salgado
Photo Editor Kathy Ryan
Publisher The New York Times
Category Photography Story/
Photojournalism, Portraits
Date February 2, 1992

KAZAKHSTAN'S
DARK
SATANIC
MILLS

A PHOTO ESSAY
BY
SEBASTIÃO
SALGADO

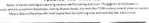

TENDING THE MACHINE

FROM METALWORK, POLLUTION

FOR BULLETS AND GAS TANKS

AIR THAT STINGS THE EYES

IN THE FURNACE ROOM, A BREATHER

VISIONS OF THE 18TH CENTURY

Publication	Buzz
Award	Silver
Design Director	Charles Hess
Designer	Charles Hess
Photographer	Mary Ellen Mark
Photo Editor	Charles Hess
Publisher	Buzz, Inc.
Category	Photography Story/Photojournalism, Portraits
Date	September/October 1992

Publication	Rolling Stone
Award	Silver
Art Director	Fred Woodward
Designer	Gail Anderson
Photographer	Mary Ellen Mark
Photo Editor	Laurie Kratochvil
Publisher	Straight Arrow Publishers, Inc.
Category	Photography Story/Photojournalism, Portraits
Date	September 3, 1992

THE PRINCE OF WILD WOOD BY JON KATZ

JACK BRIAN SEARCHES THE JERSEY SHORE FOR LOVE GIRLS AND A FUTURE

PHOTOGRAPHS BY MARY ELLEN MARK

I'M GOING TO HAVE THIS GREAT SUMMER, YOU KNOW, THIS PERFECT SUMMER WHEN I HAVE MY BODY AND MY FREEDOM, AND I CAN SCREW AND EAT JUNK AND SLEEP WHENEVER I WANT. AFTER LABOR DAY, I'M CHRISTOPHER COLUMBUS. I GO BACK HOME AND STEP OFF THE END OF THE WORLD.

Publication W
Award Silver
Creative Director Dennis Freedman
Design Director Owen Hartley
Art Directors Kirby Rodriguez, Edward Leida
Designers Edward Leida, Rosalba Sierra
Photographer Michel Comte
Publisher Fairchild Publications
Category Photography Story/Photojournalism, Portraits
Date July 13, 1992

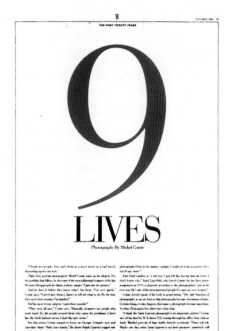

Giorgio Armani

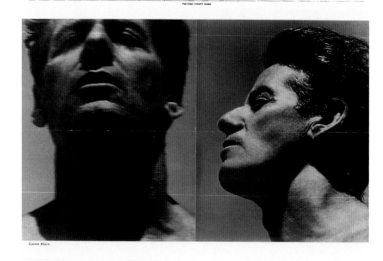

Calvin Klein

Jean Paul Gaultier

Publication	Macworld
Award	Silver
Design Director	Dennis McLeod
Art Director	Joanne Hoffman
Designer	Dennis McLeod
Photographer	Max Aguilera-Hellweg
Publisher	Macworld Communications
Category	Photography Story/Photojournalism, Portraits
Date	September 1992

THE
CREATION
OF THE
TECHNOLOGICAL
UNDERCLASS
IN
AMERICA'S
PUBLIC
SCHOOLS

Separate Realities

BY CHARLES PILLER

Photographs by
MAX AGUILERA-HELLWEG

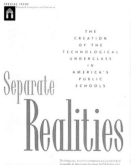

Publication	American Heritage
Award	Merit
Art Director	Peter Morance
Designer	Peter Morance
Photographer	Irving Browning
Photo Editor	Jane Colihan
Publisher	American Heritage
Category	Photography Story/Photojournalism, Portraits
Date	November 1992

Publication	Discover
Award	Merit
Art Director	David Armario
Designer	James Lambertus
Photographer	Jeffery Newbury
Photo Editor	John Barker
Publisher	Disney Magazine Publishing
Category	Photography Story/Photojournalism, Portraits
Date	May 1992

PHOTO·DISCOVERY

THE LOST CITY

by Ira Meistrich

Through boom times and grim times,
New Yorkers get on with their lives in a town
whose high, iron temper confers something of
the heroic on the least of its residents.

PHYSICISTS
with their heads in the clouds
are learning how to turn

BREAKING
THE
STORM

dangerous hailstorms
into
crop-saving
rain
showers.

ON A MORNING IN JULY it is clear and hot
in Bismarck, North Dakota...

BY KATHRYN PHILLIPS

Photography by
JEFFERY NEWBURY

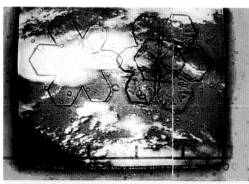

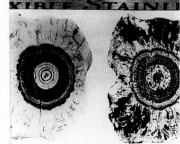

Publication Discover
Award Merit
Art Director David Armario
Designer David Armario
Photographer Hans Neleman
Photo Editor John Baker
Publisher Disney Magazine Publishing
Category Photography Story/Photojournalism, Portraits
Date August 1992

PLAYING GOD

AFTER HOURS, A PHYSICIST
AT LOS ALAMOS IS REINVENTING LIFE'S ASSEMBLY LINE,
MOLECULE BY MOLECULE.

Molding
the
Metabolism
BY DAVID H. FREEDMAN

PLAYING GOD

IF YOU WANT TO REALLY
UNDERSTAND THE NUTS AND BOLTS OF LIFE,
ARGUES JACK SZOSTAK,
WHY NOT BUILD A CELL FROM SCRATCH?

The
Handmade
Cell
BY DAVID H. FREEDMAN

PLAYING GOD

RIGHT NOW IT'S FLOATING
IN A DISH IN JAPAN. SOMEDAY IT MAY BE
OFFERING YOU ADVICE.

If He
Only Had a
Brain
BY DAVID H. FREEDMAN

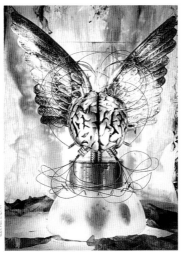

205

Publication	Entertainment Weekly
Award	Merit
Design Director	Michael Grossman
Art Director	Mark Michaelson
Designer	Miriam Campiz
Photographer	Jeffrey Thurnher
Photo Editor	Mary Dunn
Publisher	Entertainment Weekly, Inc.
Category	Photography Story/Photojournalism, Portraits
Date	February 7, 1992

Publication	Esquire
Award	Merit
Art Director	Rhonda Rubinstein
Designer	Rhonda Rubinstein
Photographer	Mary Ellen Mark
Photo Editor	Betsy Horan
Publisher	The Hearst Corporation
Category	Photography Story/Photojournalism, Portraits
Date	April 1992

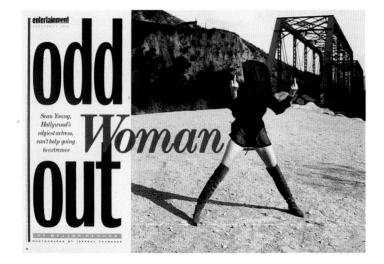

Publication Life
Award Merit
Design Director Tom Bentkowski
Photographers Chris Steele, Paul Lowe,
John Trotter,
Jean-Claud Coutausse,
Andrew Holbrooke
Photo Editor David Friend
Publisher Time/Warner, Inc.
Category Photography Story/
Photojournalism, Portraits
Date November 1992

The Unloved One

For twelve years the greatest athlete his sport has ever seen, Carl Lewis is only now becoming someone we could actually like

By Charles P. Pierce

The autograph fellows in their fine Bally gear stand busting on each other in the hallway outside the locker room. There are signatures in that room to by mined and sold like fine gold. A producer woman is headed into stage three TV pods because Carl Lewis is in that room and he can't supply what the drug snoopers need, and he's supposed to be at the studio in fifteen goddamn minutes and there ... waiting. Lives are on hold. Careers are on the line. The immediate, nervous present is scoped right down onto that hallway of Madison Square Garden, and it's bursting, waiting for the world's greatest athlete to piss in a bottle.

He's taken the icon-mold indoor long jump championship this February night, sailing off the end of a battered runway to a distance of twenty-seven feet and four and three-quarters inches. A pedestrian performance by his lofty standards but good enough, against the field. Now, with the producer woman frazzled long past TV fail-safe, he is damnable loud to catch, even in the hallways of the Garden. He blows by the fellows, signing on the fly. He comes like a firestorm, leaving his manager behind at the arena. He tells into the limo, his laugh bright brass. He's drunk so much fruit juice to insure he simple that he was here to be escorted to the gents' line, on national television. "If I call on my morning round," he says, "you'll know what's up."

He is wearing a sweet suit of his own design, the one that he wore between jumps

Photographs by Gregory Heisler

tonight. It's a billowy olive-ish thing, a wotsmy underfresh thick with hems and laced with birds of paradise peeking out through the various flora. When he jumped, he looked like the world's greatest athlete, long and lean and improbably springy in flight. In between, he looked like your great-aunt's ottoman.

This is not the stranger nor he has ever worn. That would be the uniform he helped design for the Santa Monica Track Club's green-white team at the 1991 Penn Relays in Philadelphia. Those were stars right and down, and colored to outline a shadow of the skin tone of each of the athletes. From the inside, it looked very much as if the SMTC was planning to run as track point. He teammates were along with it because if you are a number if the SMTC, you go along with Carl Lewis because he is the reason that you make all the money when you run. The SMTC he makes every time he steps on a track is the biggest reason you can make $50,000. For that, and for all the hems and for all those first-rate bandlor helds, you can put up with the race that you occasionally must perform in public in the Team Rearon in front Penn.

"I felt like the whole stadium was looking at our waving or all that," Lewis recalls, "First, I heard the buzz. Then I heard "Are they wearing anything?" Then I heard all the screms starting up "Whoa! Yeah! That's hot!" Then I missed a lot of guys staring "Shut up." The thock color are a be- a hair.

Some people never see past the clothes. Some people never see past the charging fast-cut. Some people never see past the top of nature and miraculs that his tin-sided Carl Lewis ever since he burst onto the scene in 1981, a callow 20-year-old who made the Olympic team in the long jump and the 4×100-meter relay. (Like the tree of that team, Lewis was unmarginful once beyond Lewis's doomed myth to its campaign and denied the chance to go to Moscow.) Some people never see past the flag Lewis waved at the Los Angeles Games, in 1994, ceremoniously, forgetting that there was enough reason earlier self-aggrandizement in those Olympics to ncumcen's Regor Rabe. But we past the flat there, past he just a moment, and you can gaze at a watching very much like ours.

A 31-mandable old for a compet lift in his winter, Lewis will go to the Barcelona Summer Games and lie at least want money to win three more gold medals, which would give him nine in his career. "Nobody had ever won the Olympic 105-meter twice, Lewis is going to three in a row last August, at the World Championships in Tokyo, he recaptured the world record at that distance, running at an astishing 9.86, in a race in which the two-three finishers went under the altered world record. He also put up three of the six long jumps in excess of twenty-eight feet in human history, and Mike Powell had to break Bob Bearmon's epochal twenty-three-year-old world record of twenty-nine...

"Carl's line an easy," says Leroy Burrell, her Santa Monica teammate, whose passing 100-meter record Lewis broke right in front of him, in Tokyo. "He is the single greatest athlete that track and field has ever produced."

Powell understands that as well. He has said that, world record be damned, he won't be fully validated as an athlete while in the Santa Carl Lewis in the Olympic Games. Lewis is a staggering career, so far beyond that of any other track athlete that all is regains is some ludicrous.

Still.

There is always a "still" with him. Onate, early on, Lewis manager attempted to acquire him, with Michael Jackson. That was something less than accurate. In terms of public affection, Lewis has made it as high as Jermaine, maybe. Or Tito. In 1984, Michael Jackson was selling 2,000 records a minute. Meanwhile, Lewis would run four gold medals in Los Angeles—the Jesse Owens grand slam—but his classroom audience was as off-putting as his talent was dazzling. He would not just run and jump. He would sing, too. He would act. He would be a television star. He carried by the prevailing cultural Zeitgeist, he would have it all.

Urban athletes bridled at his confidence. The studio free-and-no-how carefully he appeared to have programmed his success, from his bony-ann funeral to the flip he waved during his victory laps. The simple pathos aimed at him without mercy. Ironically, this do-or-he sees, the less popular he became. At the press conference after the 1984 Olympic 4×100-meter relay, two of Carl's teammates looked very much as if they wanted to take the baton and clout the new Jesse Owens right in the bazoo.

"Accidents," he continues today. "Which is. I do is lose. In 1948, Me-rooms was starving in 1950." He recked the top 3 could killed him. I had a wide interest, is he was bottomed in 36 years ani then. Then I want to the Olympic Training Center, and everybody said 'Roy, don't he-k?' It was a flat accident." Nevertheless, the perception was if no that Lewis was someone who had jumped to be true for it left the mainstream altogether. To imitate the effects of that perception, it's helpful to recall that two of Lewis's 1984 Olympic teammates were Michael Jordan and Mary Lou Retton. Retton, perky and conventional as the oatmeal, got the Wheaties box and in the ensuing years, Jordan has gone to an baseball tour to take industry. Lewis as, on the other hand, endures a British national and Italian clamody. He had a spill record at best-do.

It is not simply that his complete as an "amateur" "amateur" these days being devised as making a facility at city sport Americana athlete. And it is not merely that Olympic athletes tend to fade in and out of the public consciousness as four-year intervals. Lewis also wandered in the decade's great cultural rip, in which a separate or public rapture milled comfortably with cultural public endorsement. In the Sixties, he might have made it as a given economy. In the Eighties, well "word?" once again a presenter, he was ho-aed open with wedding tent-poisn.

He changed his bar. He dressed like a flanger. He was a...

Publication GQ
Award Merit
Creative Director Robert Priest
Designer Diana Haas
Photographer Gregory Heisler
Photo Editor Karen Frank
Publisher Condé Nast Publications
Category Photography Story/
Photojournalism, Portraits
Date July 1992

"THESE ARE THE BODIES OF THE PREVIOUS NIGHT'S DEAD."

They are wrapped in hand cloths that hide no more than the E.I. but something more. No medically significant or by the glow gas or handout of bodies in sustained consensus we said in the land—

—PAUL LOWE

"THE GUARD WAS BEATING BACK PEOPLE WHO WERE CROWDING IN TO GET FOOD."

Crazed building under to mosque, fatiguing bamboo breweries the grain not because they have immensely splintered on the step glass we because they have them as enough to fund them all. The magnitude of desensitizes wasn't help in anyone. Sometimes it's hard to capture it's an operation, a thing hard—

—ANDREW HOLBROOKE

"I THINK THIS IS A GIRL—IT'S HARD TO TELL WHEN THEY ARE SO SKELETAL."

Another, who was about 13 years old, at a feeding center in Baidoa. She was so hungry, but death such look at food. I couldn't take, it but I shot. it and I hope. I shot—

—ANDREW HOLBROOKE

Publication Life
Award Merit
Design Director Tom Bentkowski
Designer Marti Golon
Photographers Larry Crove, Ken Hawkins, David Buton, Rick Martin, Edd Carreon, Peter Turnley, Gary Gopp, Michael Schumann, Mark Richards, Bob Witkowski
Photo Editor Barbara Baker Burrows, Celia Waters
Publisher Time/Warner, Inc.
Category Photography Story/Photojournalism, Portraits
Date June 1992

Publication Life
Award Merit
Design Director Tom Bentkowski
Designer Marti Golon
Photographer Cristina Grarica Rodero
Photo Editor Mary Shea
Publisher Time/Warner, Inc.
Category Photography Story/Photojournalism, Portraits
Date August 1992

Publication Rolling Stone
Award Merit
Art Director Fred Woodward
Designers Fred Woodward, Gail Anderson,
Catherine Gilmore-Barnes, Debra Bishop, Angela Skouras,
Geraldine Hessler
Photographer Matthew Rolston
Photo Editor Laurie Kratochvil
Publisher Straight Arrow Publishers, Inc.
Category Photography Story/Photojournalism, Portraits
Date November 12, 1992

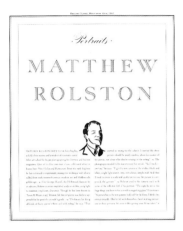

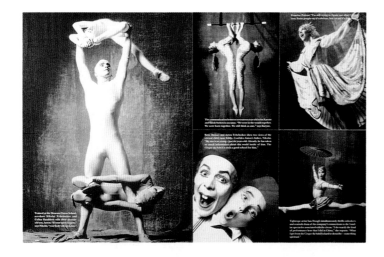

Publication San Francisco Focus
Award Merit
Art Director Mark Ulriksen
Designer Mark Ulriksen
Photographer Frank Ockenfels 3/Outline
Publisher KQED, Inc.
Category Photography Story/ Photojournalism, Portraits
Date July 1992

Publication Spin
Award Merit
Art Director Stephen Webster
Designer Maxwell Hudson
Photographer Maxwell Hudson
Photo Editor Shana Sobel
Publisher Camouflage Associates
Category Photography Story/ Photojournalism, Portraits
Date October 1992

Publication Newsweek
Award Merit
Design Director Alex Ha
Art Director Patricia Bradbury
Photographer Romano Cagnoni
Publisher Newsweek, Inc.
Category Photography Story/ Photojournalism, Portraits
Date March 13, 1992

WHAT HAPPENED TO AUDEN

W. H. Auden, photographed by Richard Avedon on St. Mark's Place in New York City, 1960.

REFLECTIONS

THE CHILDREN OF MALCOLM

by Marshall Frady

Malcolm X, photographed by Richard Avedon in New York City, 1963.

THE THEATRE

ASTONISHMENTS AND PRATFALLS

by John Lahr

Robert Lepage as Jean Cocteau, photographed by Richard Avedon in New York City, December 11, 1992.

INTERNATIONAL

PHOTO JOURNAL

Life Among the Ruins

Publication The New Yorker
Award Merit
Designers Wynn Dan, Caroline Mailhot
Photographer Richard Avedon
Publisher Advance Publications
Category Photography Story/ Photojournalism, Portraits
Date November 2, 1992
October 12, 1992
December 28, 1992

Publication	Texas Monthly
Award	Merit
Design Director	D.J. Stout
Art Director	D.J. Stout
Designer	D.J. Stout
Photographer	Dan Winters
Photo Editor	D.J. Stout
Publisher	Texas Monthly
Category	Photography Story/Photojournalism, Portraits
Date	June 1992

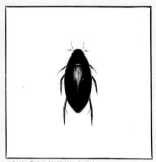

Publication	Texas Monthly
Award	Merit
Design Director	D.J. Stout
Art Director	D.J. Stout
Designer	D.J. Stout
Photographer	Mary Ellen Mark
Photo Editor	D.J. Stout
Publisher	Texas Monthly
Category	Photography Story/Photojournalism, Portraits
Date	March 1992

Publication	Texas Monthly
Award	Merit
Design Director	D.J. Stout
Art Director	D.J. Stout
Designer	D.J. Stout
Photographer	Keith Carter
Photo Editor	D.J. Stout
Publisher	Texas Monthly
Category	Photography Story/Photojournalism, Portraits
Date	January 1992

HERE'S TO THE SMALL-TOWN RODEO —PART CONTEST, PART PAGEANT, PART HARD KNOCKS AND HARD TRUTHS.

BY SKIP HOLLANDSWORTH

DOG GHOSTS AND BOTTLE TREES

WHEREVER HE LOOKS, EAST TEXAS PHOTOGRAPHER KEITH CARTER FINDS MOJO MAGIC
BY JAN JARBOE

DOG GHOST

BENT MAN

MOJO HANDS

SCARECROW

PEOPLE IN RURAL TEXAS TODAY HAVE ABOUT AS MUCH CONTACT WITH COWBOY LIFE AS DO PEOPLE IN CITIES.

BOTTLE TREES ARE LIKE DOG GHOSTS. BOTH ARE VESSELS FOR SPIRITS.

DOMINOES

BOTTLE TREE

GARLIC

Publication Time
Award Merit
Design Director Arthur Hochstein
Art Director Rudy Hoglund
Photographer Ron Auiu
Photo Editor Michele Stephenson
Publisher Time Inc. Magazine Company
Category Photography Story/Photojournalism, Portraits
Date April 12, 1992

Publication Time
Award Merit
Design Director Arthur Hochstein
Art Director Rudolph C. Hoglund
Photographers Anthony Suou, Margaret Bourke, P. F. Bentley
Photo Editor Michele Stephenson
Publisher Time Inc. Magazine Company
Category Photography Story/Photojournalism, Portraits
Date November 2, 1992

Publication Art & Auction
Award Merit
Art Director David O'Connor
Designer David O'Connor
Photographer Rob Kinmonth
Publisher Art & Auction Joint Ventures
Category Photography /Story
Date May 1992

Publication Los Angeles Times Magazine
Award Merit
Art Director Nancy Duckworth
Designer Carol Wakano
Photographer Dauna Whitehead
Photo Editor Lisa Thackaberry
Publisher Los Angeles Times
Category Photography Story/Photojournalism, Portraits
Date July 19, 1992

The "M" Word

ARTISTS LIKE TO TALK—ABOUT ANYTHING, IT
SEEMS, EXCEPT THE MARKET.
BUT HERE, FOUR OF THEM SHARE
THEIR VIEWS ON THE SUBJECT
WITH JUDD TULLY.
PHOTOGRAPHS BY ROB KINMONTH

Publication	Vogue
Award	Silver
Art Director	Raul Martinez
Designer	Eric Pryor
Photographer	Raymond Meier
Photo Editor	Esin Goknar
Publisher	Condé Nast Publishing Co., Inc.
Category	Photography Story/Still Life, Interiors, Travel
Date	November 1992

big bird

**It's an American institution, a holiday favorite.
But is it actually edible?
Jeffrey Steingarten yields to seasonal pressure
and finds the slowest and fastest ways
to cook a turkey**

My second favorite Thanksgiving dinner happened eighteen years ago inside a tiny Saab. My friends and I had never shone more brightly than on that Thursday morning as the three of us set off from Manhattan for our friends' farm in upstate New York. But two hours later, in a blinding blizzard made of snowflakes the size of dinner plates, our car involuntarily left the highway and hurtled, headlights first, onto a snowdrift that could have hidden a small suburban house. We ransacked the car for a shovel but could find nothing beyond the plum pie, the pumpkin pie, the apple pie, the two loaves of bread, and the quart of ancient Scotch that were to have been our contribution to the Thanksgiving feast.

Quickly calculating that we had enough gasoline to keep the car's heater running for two weeks, we gave up the goal of reaching upstate New York and, trying the Swiss Army knife and Norris caps without which we never traveled more than a few feet from our apartments in those days, made fast and thankful work of the pies, bread, and Scotch. A brief nap followed. We awoke to find our snowdrift enfolded in a velvet and cloudless evening rich with gas stations, tow trucks, and detailed instructions for driving back to the safety of Manhattan, just in time for a late supper at one of its excellent restaurants.

One admirable feature of my second favorite Thanksgiving dinner is that it was turkeyless. The *Oxford English* Dictionary defines turkey as "a well-known, large gallinaceous bird...now valued as a table fowl in all civilized lands." I couldn't disagree more. We eat turkey on Thanksgiving because turkey is an edible symbol, not because it is a contender at the table. It stands for the discovery of the foodstuffs of the New World and the brotherhood offered by Native Americans to those who would soon displace and even slaughter them. Edible symbols are rarely gastronomically rewarding, though I did once eat a superb dark chocolate Eiffel Tower, and a swan molded from first-rate chopped liver. If turkey were not a symbol, we would never eat as many of them as we do. Its meat is nearly always bland and stringy, and its shape is entirely incorrect.

The best part of a roast turkey is its skin. Modern turkey breeders, responding to an apparent demand for more white and less dark meat, have developed a bird consisting mainly of a huge, nearly spherical breast and short, skinny legs and thighs. Yet the breast of the bird is surely its least savory part, and its spherical shape is surely a mistake. Remember what we learned in high school about spheres? Of all geometric figures, the sphere has the lowest ratio of surface to volume; a spherical turkey, therefore, has the lowest ratio of skin to meat. It would be much better to have bred the modern turkey in the form, say, of a two-foot pizza with little wings and legs on the circumference and two broad surfaces of delicious, crackling, savory, golden roast skin with very little meat inside.

Beneath its blackened shell, Thompson's Turkey bursts with flavor. For details, see recipe.

Photographer: Raymond Meier

314

---

big bird

Even as a symbol, the turkey falls short in at least four ways:

1. The Pilgrims probably did not eat turkey at the first Thanksgiving dinner in 1621. The only firsthand account of the feast, reprinted in the Plimoth Plantation's *Thanksgiving Primer*, does not mention turkey. According to Evan Jones in *American Food*, the Pilgrims dined on venison, roast duck, roast goose, clams, eels, corn, beans, wheat and corn breads, leeks, watercress, wild plums, and homemade wine. It is doubtful that the banqueters even had thanksgiving in mind.

2. The Indians did not consciously feed the Pilgrims in their devastating first year on these shores or introduce them to terrific New World foodstuffs. According to Waverley Root and Richard de Rochemont, Native Americans did feed the colonists in Virginia, thus saving their lives, but those in Massachusetts were more suspicious. "It was an Indian habit to store away caches of long-lasting foods in various places where they might one day be needed; it was the Pilgrims' good luck to stumble on one of these caches, which kept them alive (some of them over their first terrible winter," they write in *Eating in America*.

3. Even if the Pilgrims did eat turkey at the first "Thanksgiving dinner" in 1621, they had certainly tasted much finer turkeys back home in England. The turkey, of course, originated not in Turkey but in the New World, where there were several related species. In Massachusetts they long been domesticated by the Aztecs when the Spanish conquistadors discovered Mexico in 1518; they brought the Mexican turkey back to Europe, where it was soon raised commercially. In a cookbook of 1615, *The English Huswife*, turkey appears nearly as often as chicken; it was surely familiar to the Pilgrims when they arrived here and found the Eastern wild turkey, a species inferior to the domesticated Mexican but a turkey nonetheless.

Between the time they landed in December of 1620 and their feast nearly a year later, the Pilgrims undoubtedly ate wild turkey, even if they forewent the large gallinaceous fowl at the famous feast itself. Wild game was so plentiful in North America that some writers attribute the success of colonization to its availability. Others believe that the inexhaustible plenitude of wild game, including turkeys, gave rise to the American obsession with meat, which, according to Waverley Root, astonished European visitors for two centuries.

So the turkey really symbolizes embattled carnivorous behavior and the cardiac problems that it brings. The true meaning of the Thanksgiving menu lies in the garnishes, not in the main course—in the uniquely New World cranberry, pumpkin, sweet potatoes, corn, beans, and other treasures the Europeans found growing here. That's why I consider it a quasi-religious duty to consume a generous range and amount of chocolate on this holiday. You can't give thanks without it.

4. The turkey got its silly name through two or three mistakes. You might guess that the name stemmed from a mistaken belief that Columbus had landed in Asia. You would be wrong. When the Spanish brought the turkey back home only twenty-six years after Columbus's first voyage, Europeans confused it with the guinea fowl, a distinct bird of African origin known to Aristotle and Pliny, and gave it whatever name they already applied to the guinea fowl. For the English, this was "turkey" because they believed that the African bird had come to Europe through lands controlled by the Turks; now the Aztec bird became a "turkey," too. The Germans called both the old African and new Mexican fowl *calecutische Hahn* or *Calcutta hen* (similar to the Dutch *kalkoen*), and the French named it *coq d'Inde* or simply *d'Inde*, which then became the modern *dinde*—all of these meaning the bird of India. To the Europeans, Turkey and India were more or less in the same neighborhood.

All of this is, of course, a futile exercise in ornithology. The turkey, however imperfect in taste and texture, however sloppy as a national symbol, however misnamed, is gastronomically inevitable, if not in every year then in most of them. After all, the savory and educational garnishes go quite well with a bland and golden bird; we derive communal pleasure from splitting up one gigantic object among eight or fifteen people and in eating the same thing as everybody else in the nation; and when properly roasted, the crisp, rendered, intensely flavored skin of a turkey is bested only by that of a roast suckling pig.

And that is why my first favorite Thanksgiving dinner was a Thompson's Turkey. The problem is that I've never eaten a properly prepared Thompson's Turkey—even though I've followed Thompson's instructions with slavish and obsessive care on several occasions.

Morton Thompson was a newspaperman in the 1930s and 1940s with columns in the *New York Journal* and the Hollywood *Citizen-News* (though he is more famous for his best-selling novel, *Not As a Stranger*, published in 1954 and later made into a movie). Sometimes Thompson wrote about food, and one November in the mid-1930s he gave an elaborate recipe for turkey, a recipe that has been republished often in the years that followed, turning up in pamphlets and in the popular press every ten or fifteen years since his death. You might say that the followers of Thompson's Turkey constitute something of a cult (albeit a small and benign cult) whose members differ from the population at large only in their eagerness to expend eight or ten hours of backbreaking labor to make an exceptional, a uniquely savory, turkey.

Thompson's Turkey has become such a tradition in one branch of my wife's family that the *Nashville Banner* ran a story twelve years ago about her cousin Bonnie Lloyd (the former Miss Utah), her husband, Bill, their six children, Ivey, Tiffany, Shelly, Marty, Westy, and Merrilee, and their Thompson's Turkey. It was Bill who first offered me a glimpse of Thompson's Turkey with a torn and tattered article from a 1957 *Gourmet* magazine and a quote from Robert Benchley.

Several years ago I ate a turkey prepared and roasted by Morton Thompson. I didn't eat the whole turkey, but that wasn't my fault. There were outsiders present who tattoed up on me... I will just say that I decided at that time that Morton Thompson was the greatest man since [Bride of] Saturn, and (or all I know, forearm wasn't as good as Morton Thompson.

To make a Thompson's Turkey, you first mix up Thompson's elaborate stuffing, sew it tight into a very large turkey, and brown the bird briefly at a very high temperature. Then you paint it with a paste of flour, egg, and onion juice, dry it in the oven, and paint it again, repeating this until the bird is hermetically sealed under a stiff crust. You slowly roast the ▶ 360

The remains of the day

▶ 360

Publication	Elle Decor
Award	Silver
Art Director	Caroline Bowyer
Designers	Caroline Bowyer, Jo Hay
Photographer	Raymond Meier
Publisher	Hachette Magazines, Inc.
Category	Photography Story/Still Life, Interiors, Travel
Date	August/September 1992

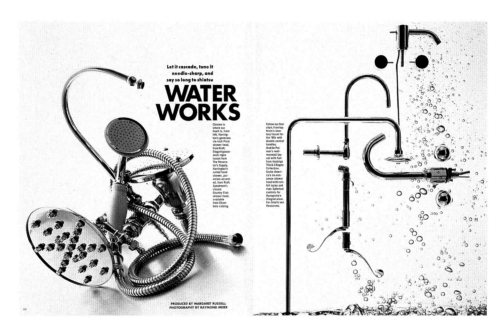

Publication Esquire
Award Silver
Design Director Rhonda Rubinstein
Art Director Rhonda Rubinstein
Designer Rhonda Rubinstein
Photographer Geof Kern
Publisher The Hearst Corporation
Category Photography Story/Still Life,
Interiors, Travel
Date March 1992

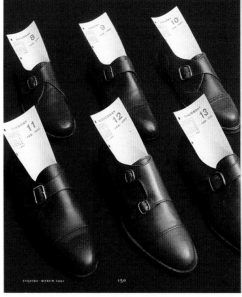

Publication	Condé Nast Traveler
Award	Silver
Design Director	Diana LaGuardia
Art Director	Christin Gangi
Designer	Audrey Razgaitis
Photographer	Richard Misrach
Photo Editor	Kathleen Klech
Publisher	Condé Nast Publishing Co., Inc.
Category	Photography Story/Still Life, Interiors, Travel
Date	March 1992

On reaching nirvana

Baja
California

AS I approach the sister towns of Cabo San Lucas and San José del Cabo, the houses turn elegant, the purple sea appears. I enter the refuge of the Hotel Palmilla, near San José, where the first thing I do is take a nap. When I wake up, the sky is a veil of angry gray. I will not, however, be dissuaded from a walk on the beach, so I set off on miles of deserted blond sand. Down the coast is Land's End, where the Sea of Cortés and the Pacific Ocean merge. The earth comes to a conclusion until you reach Antarctica, unless you stop in at Easter Island. There is no reason to hurry. I'm here to do nothing. This I repeat like an incantation. I concentrate on breathing air so pure I have a momentary dizzy spell.

I eat: fish soup with olive oil, guacamole, beans in cheese, seafood enchiladas, a beer.

Back on the terrace, in the dark, I watch the relentless assault of the ocean against the beach. Ten minutes pass. I take off my wristwatch.

PHOTOGRAPHS BY
RICHARD MISRACH   133

Day 1, Arrival: A room, a storm, disorientation. Clouds lift, land ends. Fish soup and olive oil

Day 2, Adjustment: Bleary dawn, patience, pelicans. A nap without time. Fragrance of lime. Shrimp

A BLEARY dawn and a hurricane-force gale. The palm fronds are doing a Saint Vitus' dance. Around eleven, the weather improves but remains cloudy. I discover that light isn't just blue ocean under blinding sun. It is also melted silver with a pencil-thin band of gold along the horizon. It is anthracite and slate and, toward the distant equator, mottled copper and shards of gold.

I also discover that one can spend eternity watching birds. They can teach patience, quiescence. One pelican stands immobile for a very long time, his humped profile sculpted against the sky. Under his eye, I stretch out on the sand and lose track of time. Having accomplished this, I'm unduly proud of myself.

My hotel is nirvana. Why leave? *Là, tout n'est qu'ordre et beauté; luxe, calme, et volupté.* Still, at night I drive to San José. A bell chimes every fifteen minutes. From the loudspeaker come the sounds of the Gipsy Kings doing "My Way." The fragrance of lime is everywhere. Filled with shrimp and alcohol, I sleep like a baby.

135

219

Publication Bride's & Your New Home
Award Merit
Art Director Phyllis Richmond Cox
Designer Anne Bigler
Photographer Michael Geiger
Publisher Condé Nast Publishing Co., Inc.
Category Photography Story/Still Life, Interiors, Travel
Date December 1992/January 1993

Publication Condé Nast Traveler
Award Merit
Design Director Diana La Guardia
Art Director Christin Gangi
Designer Mike Powers
Photographer Keith Carter
Photo Editor Kathleen Klech
Publisher Condé Nast Publishing Co., Inc.
Category Photography Story/Still Life, Interiors, Travel
Date February 1992

FINE DESIGNS...
SET A TABLE WITH
ARTISTIC STYLE

AROUND
the
BEND

Welcome to the desert, brother. You're in Big Bend now. Just hills and mesas and open land clear down to the churning Rio Grande. This is one stretch of southwest Texas even Texans rarely see, but that is their mistake. Ride the hills, raft the river, and marvel, as you do, that this moonscape is a national park

This is hard country, the locals warn, and you have to love it to stay

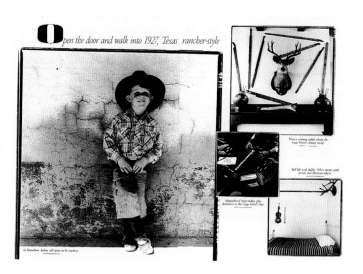

Open the door and walk into 1927, Texas rancher-style

It's good morning for Vietnam. Pico Iyer finds it awakening to its place in the world

A delicate innocence

PHOTOGRAPHS BY BRIGITTE LACOMBE

A world within a world. A monk prepares for prayers.

Shortly before midnight, the taxi dancers stream out in party dresses — Saigon is like a giant cathedral of the profane

The difference is that in Vietnam you cannot spend money if you want to; in Saigon you cannot save it

Publication Condé Nast Traveler
Award Merit
Design Director Diana La Guardia
Art Director Christin Gangi
Photographer Brigitte Lacombe
Photo Editor Kathleen Klech
Publisher Condé Nast Publishing Co., Inc.
Category Photography Story/
Still Life, Interiors, Travel
Date January 1992

Publication Elle Décor
Award Merit
Art Director Caroline Bowyer
Designers Caroline Bowyer, Jo Hay
Photographer Raymond Meier
Publisher Hachette Magazines, Inc.
Category Photography Story/
Still Life, Interiors, Travel
Date December 1991/January 1992

CLEARLY FESTIVE

CLEARLY FESTIVE

CLEARLY FESTIVE

Publication Elle Décor
Award Merit
Art Director Caroline Bowyer
Designers Caroline Bowyer, Jo Hay
Photographer Andrew Eccles
Publisher Hachette Magazines, Inc.
Category Photography Story/
Still Life, Interiors, Travel
Date June/July 1992

Translated from the English

On the terraces of their Provençal villa, Claus Scheinert and Tom Parr cultivate an expatriate tradition. By Mac Griswold

Photographs by Jerry Harpur

Some of the nicest people we know live in perfect harmony with their chairs. From straightforward function to wild eccentricity, celebrity seating is always a matter of style

Celebrity Seating

Profound—if unlikely—echoes of English arts and crafts gardens can still be heard in Provence

This is the sort of place Ernest de Ganay once called a "gentleman of a garden...whom one constantly re-discovers."

Publication House and Garden
Award Merit
Creative Director Dania Martinez Davey
Photographer Jerry Harpur
Photo Editor Susan Goldberger
Publisher Condé Nast Publishing Co., Inc.
Category Photography Story/
Still Life, Interiors, Travel
Date March 1992

Publication	Martha Stewart Living
Award	Merit
Design Director	Gael Towey
Art Director	Jennifer Warerek
Photographer	Grant Peterson
Publisher	Time Publishing Ventures
Category	Photography Story/Still Life, Interiors, Travel
Date	February/March 1992

cakes

Five delicious, beautiful, homemade confections.

When we remember special days, it seems there was always a cake. Birthdays, weddings, anniversaries, going-away parties, welcome-home parties. There were lopsided cakes with patchy frosting, and cakes with decorations so elaborate they must have taken a week (a sure sign that what was beneath wouldn't taste very good). But each marked an occasion as special. Now we bring you five cakes that would make any old day a celebration. All are delicious and utterly beautiful, with decorations that can be finished for to the cake itself stays fresh. Most of the frostings, fillings, and step-by-step instructions for assembling and decorating are on the next nine pages; for the rest, and for the basic batters, see the recipe section in the back of the magazine.

PHOTOGRAPHS BY GRANT PETERSON

Publication	Harper's Bazaar
Award	Gold
Creative Director	Fabien Baron
Art Director	Joel Berg
Designer	Johan Svensson
Photographer	Peter Lindbergh
Publisher	The Hearst Corporation
Category	Photography Story/ Fashion, Beauty
Date	December 1992

"in my solitude here, I have what is needed to recharge my forces. Here, poetry exudes from everywhere.... One has only to drift away into a dream to find inspiration."
—Paul Gauguin

Photographed by Peter Lindbergh

"All her features had a Raphaelesque harmony at the point where their curves met, her mouth modelled by a sculptor for speaking and kissing the language of joy and suffering." Previous spread: Red and white patterned fabric from Rodeo Hula, Inc. Photographed at the Somerset Falls, Jamaica. Opposite page: Striped silk organza peasant blouse, about 1993, from Yves Saint Laurent Rive Gauche. On lips: deep but transparent colors; Sheer Conditioning Lipstick #8. Eyes are defined with kohl of Lelume Pencil in Black. Both by Yves Saint Laurent. This page: Orange, green, and yellow striped long skirt from Christian Lacroix Prêt-a-Porter.

"The silence of the night in Tahiti is ... absolute. Nothing else exists; there is not even the cry of a bird to break the quiet.... I can feel all this permeating me, and at this moment I feel a sense of total repose." Purple and ivory fabric from Radio Hula, Inc. Bare necessity: Neutrogena's Sesame Seed Body Oil.

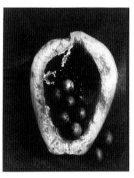

"I had been seduced ...by this land and by its simple and primitive people. To create something new, it is necessary to go back to the sources, to the infancy of humanity...." Opposite page: White jacquard organza floor-length shirt, about $550, by Randolph Duke. Chalk-free color from Clinique's Sheer Intensities line: Grapeskin Soft-Pressed Eye Shadow and Plum Bronze Young Face Powder Blusher echo the depth and richness of glorious, sun-warmed fruit. Voluptè Body Lotion by Oscar de la Renta with notes of melon, citrus, and exotic flowers soothes and moisturizes, enveloping skin in the scent of tropical nights.

Publication Details
Award Silver
Art Director B.W. Honeycutt
Designer Markus Kiersztan
Photographer Hugh Hales-Tooke
Photo Editor Greg Pond
Publisher Condé Nast Publishing Co., Inc.
Category Photography Story/Fashion, Beauty
Date December 1992

Publication	Harper's Bazaar
Award	Silver
Creative Director	Fabien Baron
Art Director	Joel Berg
Designer	Johan Svensson
Photographer	Patrick Demarchelier
Publisher	The Hearst Corporation
Category	Photography Story/Fashion, Beauty
Date	November 1992

Out
on the ocean,
away from it all,
still you always travel
in style; all spare, chic and
unstudied glamour. This page:
Yellow silk caftan, worn over matching
silk slim pants, about $3,960, the outfit by
Bill Blass. Opposite page: White nylon Lycra
maillot with thin spaghetti straps, about $97, by
Isaac Mizrahi. Eyeglasses, Robert Marc Opticians, NYC.

Publication	Details
Award	Merit
Art Director	B.W. Honeycutt
Designer	Markus Kiersztan
Photographer	Enrique Badulescu
Photo Editor	Greg Pond
Publisher	Condé Nast Publishing Co., Inc.
Category	Photography Story/Fashion, Beauty
Date	August 1992

Publication	Details
Award	Merit
Art Director	B.W. Honeycutt
Designer	Markus Kiersztan
Photographer	Albert Watson
Photo Editor	Greg Pond
Publisher	Condé Nast Publishing Co., Inc.
Category	Photography Story/Fashion, Beauty
Date	July 1992

Publication	Details
Award	Merit
Art Director	B.W. Honeycutt
Designer	Markus Kiersztan
Photographer	Guzman
Photo Editor	Greg Pond
Publisher	Condé Nast Publishing Co., Inc.
Category	Photography Story/Fashion, Beauty
Date	April 1992

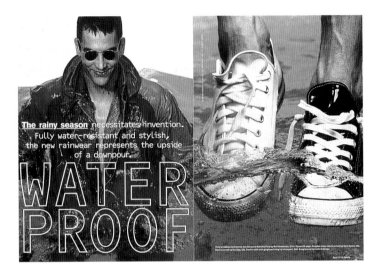

index

Design Directors

STUDIOS

Art Directors

PUBLISHERS

illustrators

DESIGNERS

PHOTOGRAPHERS

PHOTO EDITORS

Publications

CLIENTS

Creative Directors

Baron, Fabien 47, 48, 72, 80, 81, 88, 89, 90, 92, 93, 126, 127, 128, 197, 224, 227

Feiterouf, Laurie 100
Freedman, Dennis 27, 202,

Hunter, Kent 64

Martinez Davey, Dania 222

Priest, Robert 158, 182, 184, 207

Design Directors

Albright, Alex 50
Armario, David 85, 86
Askwith, John 173, 196

Baron, Fabien 89, 93
Bauman, Mary K. 150
Balkind, Audrey 64
Bentkowski, Tom 50, 94, 129, 207, 208
Bernard, Walter 78, 106
Best, Robert 24, 95
Bierut, Michael 43, 52, 91, 104
Bodkin, Tom 35, 71
Brooks, R. Lloyd 100
Bucchianeri, Alberto 27, 51, 139, 140

Carson, David 25, 82, 96
Charton, Aldona 69
Chung, Percy 109
Cook, Ken 188
Cumomo, Yolanda 185

Depaule, Jean Charles 55
Doherty, Melanie 62
Dorr, Cheri 65
Drenttel, Bill 59, 60
Duggan, Paula 108

Fernandes, Teresa 174
Froelich, Janet 119

Garlan, Judy 124, 156, 169
Geismar, Daphne 29

George, Roberts J. 173
Giovanitti, Sara 77
Glaser, Milton 53, 78, 106, 144
Grossman, Michael 20, 46, 86, 87, 125, 148, 149, 157, 171, 184, 206

Ha, Alex 211
Hartley, Owen 27, 202
Helfand, Jessica 164
Hess, Charles 200
Hindrichs, Kit 48, 76, 94, 128
Hochbaum, Susan 59
Hochstein, Arthur 18, 26, 27, 137, 214
Hoffman, Steven 26, 99, 134, 155, 186
Honeycutt, B.W 85,
Hopkins, Will 150
Hornall, John 54
Hunter, Kent 64

Jaffe, Holly 84
Jean-Louis, Galie 30, 114, 115

Kefauver, Will 106
Kelly, Paula 56
Kner, Andrew 28
Koepke, Gary 41, 61, 100, 113, 114, 138
Koudys, Mark 54, 110, 145
Koura, Andrea 109
Kowal, Nancy 151

La Guardia, Diana 27, 124, 125, 148, 149, 151, 169, 219, 220, 221
La Pine, Julia 55
Leeds, Greg 163
Lupi, Italo 156

Marshall, Mary 102
Martinez Davey, Dania 185
McLeod, Dennis 188, 195, 203
McNeill, Joe 107
Miller, J.Abbott 40
Mitchell, Patrick 75, 88
Morla, Jennifer 65
Munoz, Beatrice 185

Newman, Robert 35, 115, 162, 163

Orr, David 111

Parham, John 64
Pedersen, B. Martin 28, 104, 105, 121, 141, 142, 143, 144, 187, 188
Petrick, Robert 79, 111

Pospischil, Hans-Georg 175
Poulin, Richard 62
Priest, Robert 195

Rae, Erena 28
Ramsay, Bruce 56, 110
Rank, Jerry J. 84
Renfro, Doug 174, 185
Roberts, Eva 50
Rowntree, Dirk 33
Rubinstein, Rhonda 87, 218
Rushworth, John 53

Saint-Loubert Bié, Jérome 55
Sanford, John Lyle 29
Scher, Paula 59, 60
Scopin, Joseph W. 116
Shannon, Susanna 55
Shostak, Mitch 96
Staley, Lynn 70
Stout, D.J. 135, 136, 212, 213

Towey, Gael 49, 123, 130, 131, 223

Wilson, Fo 25

Ziff, Lloyd 90, 91, 177

Art Directors

Armario, David 74, 85, 86, 113, 162, 170, 183, 204, 205
Armus, Jill 25
Aziza-Ooka, Dian 180

Bacchus, Derek 20, 29
Baker, Richard 34, 119, 154, 165, 197
Bartholomay, Lucy 31, 67, 117, 164
Becker, Syndi 24
Bentkowski, Tom 93
Berg, Joel 47, 48, 72, 80, 81, 88, 89, 90, 92, 93, 126, 127, 128, 197, 224, 227
Bernard, Walter 53, 144
Berry, Pamela 138, 187
Bierut, Michael 91
Bonavita, Donna 146, 188
Bonziglia, Alex 69
Bowyer, Caroline 45, 217, 221, 222
Bradbury, Patricia 22, 23, 148, 150, 211

Brewer, Linda 35, 71, 89
Bundi, Renee 107

Carson, David 96, 159
Carstensen, Paul 111, 113, 145, 162
Charlton, Aldona 69
Chung, Fani 63
Chung, Percy 109
Chwast, Seymour 105, 106
Clark, Liz 108
Cohen, Nancy 95, 131, 132

Danzig, Mark 194
DiLorenzo, Lou 100, 137, 196
Doe, Kelly 165
Doyle, Stephen 60
Drace, Matthew 49, 94, 95, 185
Duckworth, Nancy 21, 31, 118, 215
Duggan, Paula 108
Dzienciol, Jeanne 194

Easler, Jaimey 48, 76, 94, 128
Ellis, Jan 58, 63, 111, 112, 189
Ellis, Laurie 58, 63, 111, 112, 189
Erger-Fass, Carole 101

Fabella, Ted 103
Fedele, Gene 51
Fernandes, Teresa 174
Ford, Scott 66
Fox, Bert 164
Frankel, Margot 90, 91
Froelich, Janet 32, 33, 71, 118, 119, 146, 147, 164, 168, 177, 189,
190, 191, 192, 197, 198, 199
Frost, Vince 53

Gangi, Christin 124, 125, 148, 149, 169, 219, 220, 221
Garlan, Judy 124, 156, 169
Gartland, Mark 45
Gassner, Christof 133
Gee, Earl 63
Geismar, Daphne 28
Glaser, Milton 53

Harrigan, Laura 130
Helfand, Jessica 35
Hinrichs, Kit 48, 76, 94, 128
Hochbaum, Susan 59
Hodgson, Michael 58
Hoffman, Joanne 161, 188, 195, 203
Hoglund, Rudolph C. 18, 26, 27, 137, 214
Honeycutt, B.W. 85, 157, 166,

183, 226, 228, 229
Hornall, John 55
Houser, David W. 133

Isley, Alexander 52, 103, 104, 140, 141, 161

Jaffe, Holly 84
Janerka, Andrzej 195
Jean-Louis, Galie 30, 114, 115
Johnson, Anne 123, 130

Kalish, Nicki 31
Kamenish, Gail M. 77
Kascht, John 116
Katona, Diti 57, 61
Kelly, Paula 56, 110
Kner, Andrew 28
Koepke, Gary 42, 61, 100, 113, 114, 138
Koudys, Mark 83, 88, 122
Koura, Andrea 109
Kuypers, Christiaan 67, 99, 134, 151

Lambertus, James 85, 86
LaPine, Julia 55
Lappen, Arlene 81, 148, 157
Lehmann-Haupt, Carl 95, 131, 132
Leida, Edward 202
Loewy, David 107
Lupi, Italo 156

Marshall, Mary 102
Martinez, Raul 193, 216
McFarlin, Ken 66
Menchin, Scott 84
Michaelson, Mark 20, 46, 86, 87, 125, 149, 171, 184, 206
Morance, Peter 84, 204
Morla, Jennifer 65
Motichka, Dolores 116
Muller, John 102

Nestor, Okey 65
Nicolay, Fabien 133
Niemi, Arthur 22

O'Connor, David 187, 215
Olenyik, John 106
Orr, David 111
Oudin, Jérome 54

Palecek, Jane 94, 105, 158, 172, 184
Parker, Janet 158
Pearson, Randell 28, 104, 105, 121, 141, 142, 143, 144, 187
Pedersen, B. Martin 28, 104,

105, 141, 142, 143, 144, 187, 188
Perry, F. Darrin 161, 186
Peters, Margery 150
Petrick, Robert 79, 111
Phelps, Lynn 30
Phillips, Jim 161
Pierce, Glenn 108
Piercy, Clive 58
Pinto, Andrea 107
Poulin, Richard 62
Prather, Pat 173, 196
Pylpczak, John 57, 61

Rank, Jerry J. 84
Renfro, Doug 161
Richmond Cox, Phyllis 220
Roberts, Eva 50
Rodriguez, Kirby 27, 202
Rowntree, Dirk 33
Rubinstein, Rhonda 18, 19, 22, 87, 157, 206, 218
Rushworth, John 53

Scher, Paula 60
Schneider, Sandra 30, 115
Sessa, Marsha 95
Sheehan, Nora 50, 129
Silva, Greg 96,
Slavin, Kevin 131
Smith, Bill 66
Sokolow, Rena 31, 68, 117
Staebler, Tom 159
Stearns, Sarah 176
Stermole, Rick 64
Stout, D.J. 135, 136, 212, 213
Stucki, Ron 107, 108
Suzuki, Tom 102, 103, 162, 175

Toltzis Makon, Joy 106
Towey, Gail 49
Tremain, Kerry 22
Turelli, Paula Kreiter 173, 196

Ulriksen, Mark 160, 210

Warerek, Jennifer 131, 223
Webster, Stephen 186, 210
Winters, Carole 24
Woodward, Fred 19, 38, 41, 44, 83, 97, 98, 99, 120, 159, 160, 181, 182, 185, 201, 209

Designers

Aggarwal, Sarika 138, 187
Allen, Dave 173, 196

Anderson, Gail 38, 41, 44, 97, 160, 201, 209
Appen, Allyson 180
Armario, David 74, 86, 113, 162, 183, 205
Arnett, Dana 43

Bachleda, Florian 35, 115, 163
Baker, Richard 34, 119, 154, 197
Ball, Alan 101
Bartholomay, Lucy 31, 67, 117, 164
Baseman, Frank 53, 78, 144
Bates, David 55,
Becker, Syndi 24, 95
Betts Elizabeth 46, 171
Benson, Charlene 32, 119, 189
Bentkowski, Tom 129
Best, Robert 24, 95
Betts, Elizabeth 46, 171
Bierut, Michael 43, 52, 91, 104
Bigler, Anne 220
Bishop, Debra 38, 41, 44, 97, 98, 160, 185, 209
Bonavita, Donna 146, 188
Bonziglia, Alex 69
Bowyer, Caroline 45, 217, 221, 222
Branson-Meyer, Bruce 55
Brewer, Linda 35, 189
Brooks, R. Lloyd 100
Brooks, Sharrie 65
Bucchianeri, Alberto 27, 51, 139
Bundi, Renee 107

Campiz, Miriam 46, 86, 206
Carson, David 24, 25, 82, 159
Carstensen, Paul 111, 113, 144, 162
Carter, Daniel 67, 99, 134, 151
Cerveny, Lisa 43, 91
Chapman, Scott 57
Charlton, Aldona 69
Christensen, Keith 101
Christensen, Josh 46
Chung, Fani 63
Chung, Percy 109
Clark, Liz 108
Cohen, Nancy 95, 132,
Comitini, Peter 22, 23
Cook, Timothy 102, 103
Cortez, Lynette 52, 103, 104, 140, 161
Crisp, Denise 58
Cruser, Kim 91

Dan, Wynn 211
Danzig, Mark 194

De Bevoise, Andrea 186
Del Vecchio, Kathryn 95
Depaule, Jean-Charles 55
Dettner, James 102
DeVore III, Nicholas 84
Di Lorenzo, Lou 100, 137, 174, 196
Dickens, Holly 119
Diener, Ruth 64
Dinglasan, John 162
Dixon, Charles, III 78
Doe, Kelly 34, 165
Doherty, Melanie 62
Dolan, Kathleen 188
Doyle, Stephen 60
Drace, Matthew 94, 95, 185
Duckworth, Nancy 21
Dzienciol, Jeanne 194

Egger-Schlesinger, Anna 51, 139, 140
Ellis, Jan 58, 63, 111, 112, 189
Ellis, Laurie 58, 63, 111, 112, 189

Fabella, Ted 103
Folkmann, Joan 62
Foshaug, Jackie 48, 76, 94, 128
Frey, Jane 137
Froelich, Janet 71, 191, 198
Frost, Vince 53

Gangi, Chrisin 27, 124, 149, 151
Garlan, Judy 124, 156, 169
Gartner, Craig 26, 134
Gassner, Christof 133
Gee, Earl 63
Geismar, Daphne 29
Genninger, Laura 183
Gilman, Jennifer 163
Gilmore-Barnes, Catherine 38, 41, 44, 98, 160, 209
Gilmore-Barnes, Robin 124
Giovanitti, Sara 77
Glaser, Milton 106
Gockel Dazzo, Susan 194
Goldman, David 66
Golon, Marti 94, 208
Grossman, Michael 20, 46, 149, 171
Grubaugh, Elizabeth 186
Gutierrez, Gaemer 49

Haas, Diana 158, 207
Hankinson, Steven 90
Harrigan, Laura 49
Hatlestad, Heidi 55
Hay, Jo 45, 217, 221, 222
Helfand, Jessica 164
Hess, Charles 200

Hessler, Geraldine 38, 41, 44, 160, 209
Hochbaum, Susan 59
Hodgson, Michael 58
Honeycutt, B.W. 166
Hornall, John 55
Hudson, Maxwell 210
Hunter, Kent 64

Inglis, Mark 23

Janerka, Andrzej 195
Jean-Louis, Galie 30, 114, 115
Johnson, Ann 49
Johnson, Tim 161, 188, 195
Johnson, Kate 162

Kalish, Nicki 31
Kascht, John 116
Katona, Diti 57, 61
Kelly, Paula 56, 110
Keshishian, Alicia 105
Kiersztan, Markus 85, 166, 226, 228, 229
Kobberger, Brian 183
Kono, Carol 58
Korjenek, Kelly 159
Koudys, Mark 54, 83, 88, 110, 122, 145
Koura, Andrea 109
Kuypers, Christiaan 99

Lambertus, James 85, 86, 170, 183, 204
Lambson, Don 175
LaPine, Julia 55
Lauterback, Kevin 52
Leeds, Greg 163
Lehmann-Haupt, Carl 95, 132
Leida, Edward 202
Littrell, Kandy 32, 118, 119, 146, 147, 164, 168, 177, 191, 192, 197
Loewy, David 107
Lupi, Italo 156

Mailhot, Caroline 211
Makela, P. Scott 43
Marroquin, Patricia 45
Marschall, Dorothy 94, 158, 184
Marshall, Mary 102
Mastrianni, Gregory 81
McFarlin, Ken 66
McLeod, Dennis 203
Menchin, Scott 84
Merin, Steve 51
Meyerson, Ron 23
Michals, Duane 59
Michaelson, Mark 46, 125, 184
Mikolajczyk, Tony 150

Miller, J. Abbott 40
Mitchell, Patrick 75, 88
Morance, Peter 84, 204
Morla, Jennifer 65
Motichka, Dolores 116
Muller, John 102
Munoz, Beatrice 185

Nesnadny, Joyce 88
Ng, Lian 55
Nicastro, David 51
Niemi, Arthur 22

O'Connor, David 187, 215
Ogata, Robin 66
Okamoto, Sharon 53, 78, 144
Orr, David 111
Oudin, Jerome 55

Palecek, Jane 172
Parker, Janet 158
Pedersen, B. Martin 28, 105, 121, 141, 142, 143, 144, 187, 188
Perry, F. Darrin 26, 155, 161, 186
Petrick, Robert 79, 111
Phelps, Lynn 30
Picón, Michael 148, 157
Pierce, Glenn 108
Piercy, Clive 58
Poulin, Richard 62
Powers, Mike 148, 220
Priest, Robert 182, 184, 195
Pryor, Eric 193, 216

Radeka, Dina 40
Ramm, Diddo 42, 61, 100, 113, 114, 138
Rank, Jerry J. 84
Razgaitis, Audrey 125, 169, 219
Reid, Kristin 20, 29
Ress, Laura 79, 111
Roberts, Eva 50
Rochow, Eric 84
Rohr, Dixon 148, 150
Rosen, Jonathon 24
Rota, Kathi 32, 118, 147, 177, 190, 191, 199
Rubenstein, Rhonda 18, 19, 157, 206, 218
Rushworth, John 53
Russo, Giovanni 49, 95

Saint-Loubert Bie, Jérome 55
Sanford, John Lyle 29
Scher, Paula 60
Schoenauer, Walter 177
Schrader, Julie 161
Schuckhart, Kay 141

Sessa, Marsha 95
Shannon, Suzanna 55
Sheehan, Nora 50, 129
Sierra, Rosalba 202
Silva, Greg 96
Simpkins, Rosemary 62
Simpson Greg 105, 106
Skouras, Angela 38, 41, 44, 99, 160, 181, 209
Smith, Pamela S. 174
Sokolow, Rena 31, 68, 70, 117
Staley, Lynn 70
Steele, Laura 66
Stout, D.J. 135, 136, 212, 213
Stucki, Ron 107, 108
Sumichrast, Josef 28
Svensson, Johan 47, 48, 72, 88, 89, 92, 93, 126, 127, 197, 224, 227

Taylor, Blake 101
Torres, Damon 67, 134, 151
Tremain, Kerry 22
Truscio, Ed 99, 186

Ulriksen, Mark 210

Vogler, David 67

Waerek, Jennifer 49
Wakano, Carol 215
White, W. Thomas 133
Wilson, Fo 25
Wommack, Curt 50
Wong, Anita 160
Woodward, Fred 38, 41, 44, 83, 97, 99, 120, 160, 182, 185, 209

Yee, Julie Anne 29

Ziff, Lloyd 177
Zipser, Tami 51

Illustrators

Adams, Lisa 46
Allen, Julian 174
Allen, Terry 113, 162
Asmussen, Don 116

Bachem, Paul 104
Bagge, Peter 166
Baker, Kyle 166
Barbour, Karen 124
Barry, Linda 171
Baseman, Gary 174

Billout, Guy 174
Binkley, Gina 81
Bishofs, Maris 41
Blackwell, Patrick 117
Blakeslee, Stanton 50
Botana, Federico 69
Blitt, Barry 41, 46, 149, 160, 169
Brady, Dave 69
Bralds, Braldt 41
Breeden, Paul M. 150
Brodner, Steve 41, 163
Brooks, Lou 23
Burke, Philip 35, 41, 99
Burns, Charles 41, 158, 159, 160

Camp, Bob 166
Carroll, Larry 25
Carter, Daniel 67
Calver, Steve 41
Chwast, Seymour 28, 176
Clark, Liz 108
Cerio, Steve 46
Cober, Alan E. 41, 174
Cober, Leslie 103
Coe, Sue 160
Collier, John 41, 147, 177
Cowles, Dan 166
Cax, Paul 52
Cowles, David 116
Cronin, Brian 44
Craig, John 108, 162

Daigle, Stéphan 174
Davis, Paul 41
Day, Rob 41
DeSeve, Peter 34
Dionisi, Sandra 102
Dougan, Michael 171
Doyle, Stephen 60
Draper, Chad 75
Drescher, Henrik 44
Drawson, Blair 41, 173
Dunnick, Stasys 41

Enos, Randall 174
Eidvigevicius, Stasys 41
English, Mark 41

Fiedler, Joseph Daniel 164
Flesher, Vivienne 41, 77
Field, Anne 117
Fisher, Jeffrey 157
Friedman, Drew 46, 166, 171

Gall, Chris 175
Garrett, Tom R. 30
Gee, Earl 63
Gillis, Scott 46

Glaser, Milton 41
Glidden, Joseph 114
Goldsworth, Andy 128
Goldstrom, Robert 41
Gosfield, Josh 25, 31, 41, 46, 64,
  157, 161, 171, 172, 174
Grace, Alexa 41
Graves, Keith 118
Greif, Gene 174
Grimwade, John 124, 148, 149,
  151
Guarnaccia, Steven 59, 156, 164
Guip, Amy 111, 162

Haggerty, Mick 28
Halgren, Gary 24
Hambly, Bob 117
Helnwein, Gottfried 41
Hendler, Sandra 174
Hernandez, Gilberto 166
Hersey, John 174
Holland, Brad 41
Hughes, David 165

Ilic, Mirko 106
Isip, Jordan 173

Jetter, Frances 163
Johnson, Peter 174

Kascht, John 116
Katchor, Ben 171
Kaz 166
Kelly, Ellsworth 92
Kelley, Gary 41, 156
Kern, Geof 154
Kerr, Thomas 163
Kidd, Chip 132
King, J.D. 64
Knott, Grace 46
Kroninger, Stephen 162
Kruger, Barbara 18
Kunz, Anita 22, 41, 172, 174
Kuypers, Christiaan 99

Lee, Ka-Sing 109
Lertola, Joe 27
Levine, Laura 174
Liepke, Skip 41
Linn, Warren 69
Lins, Rico 35
Lloyd, Mary Anne 174
Lopez, Nola 46, 171
Lopez-Ortiz, Dennis 44

MacDonald, Ross 103, 147, 168,
  177
Maffia, Daniel 41
Mahurin, Matt 41, 44, 96, 158,
  172

Martin, Agnes 92
Martori, Patti 33
Matsumura, Glenn 113
Mattos, John 28
Mayer, Bill 103
Mayforth, Hal 151
McGuire, Richard 59
McLean, Wilson 18
McMullan, James 41
Meckler, Ron 99
Menchin, Scott 30, 35, 115, 164
Meyers, Steve 46
Miller, Peter Read 26
Morgan, Scott 75
Morris, Rick 66

Nelson, Bill 41
Noguchi, Isamu 113

Panter, Gary 147
Payne, C.F. 41, 49, 161, 176
Paraskevas, Michael 41
Pedersen, Judy 77
Pendleton, Roy 141
Picasso, Dan 55
Pietzch, Steve 75
Piven, Hanoch 46
Pohl, David 169
Putnam, Jamie 44

Risko, Robert 41
Roberts, Scott 108
Rohrer, Dean 166
Rosen, Jonathon 24, 157, 159,
  166, 170
Russo, Anthony 31, 41, 68, 147

Sadowski, Witkor 41
Sandlin, David 147, 177
Scher, Paula 68, 108
Schwartz, Daniel 41
Shumaker, Ward 68
Smale, Brian 75
Smith, Elwood 107
Smith, Lane 41, 174
Staedman, Ralph 32, 44
Stamaty, Mark Alan 171
Stevenson 84
Stewart, J.W. 117
Studer, Gordon 96
Sugg, Andy 50
Sumichrast, Jösef 28
Summers, Mark 41
Sweeny, Glynis 30

Taccani, Silvia 161
Tanaka, Ikko 48, 76
Tanhauser, Gary 75, 158, 161
Tarlofsky, Malcolm 74, 177
Trueman, Gregg 67

Tucker, Mark 81

Ulriksen, Mark 41

Vasilakis, Anastasia 155
Velez, Ivan Jr. 166
Vellekoop, Maurice 166
Villa, Roxanna 49, 95

Wakabayashi, Greg 149, 151
Weisbecker, Philippe 77
White, Mack 166
Whitehead, Gary 107
Wilcox, David 159
Woodruff 41
Woolley, Janet 34, 41, 105, 165

Zingarelli, Mark 171

Photographers

Abranowicz, William 130
Afanador, Ruven 49, 125
Aguilera-Hellweg, Max 44, 74,
  203
Anderson, Stephen 93
Andersson, Patrik 89
Arnaud, Michel 47, 48, 89, 93
Arnold, Eve 35, 118
Art Lab, Inc. 65
Asnin, Marc 192
Astor, Josef 40
Auiu, Ron 214
Avedon, Richard 211

Badulescu, Enrique 85, 228
Baker Smith, Ron 54, 83, 110,
  122, 145
Basilion, Nick 64
Benson, Harry 94, 129
Bentley, P.F. 214
Black Star 137
Blessing Hendrich 139,
Bourke, Margaret 214,
Brakha, Moshe 118
Brown, Skip 29
Browning, Irving 204
Buck, Chris 184
Buton, David 208

Cabello, Roger 111
Cagnoni, Romano 211
Caraeff, Ed, 208
Carreon, Edd 208
Carter, Keith 71, 135, 213, 220
Chernush, Kay 145
Chung, Percy 109

Clement, Michelle 143, 188
Comte, Michel 202
Corbijn, Anton 186
Coutausse, Jean-Claude 207
Crosby, Tim 196
Crove, Larry 208

Davies and Starr 49, 74, 123
Dauman, Henri 114
Delsol, Michael 87
Demarchelier, Patrick 47, 48,
  72, 80, 90, 126, 128, 227
Department of Special
  Collections, Syracuse
  University Library; Courtesy
  of Magaret Bourke-White
  Estate 137
Douglas Brothers, The 53, 114
Duke, William 31
Dykinga, Jack 196

Eccles, Andrew 91, 118, 191,
  222
Endress, John Paul 43
Erler, Glen 96, 187
Estine, Darryl 86
Everett Collection 94

Fellman, Sandi 59
Ferrato, Donna 185
FPG International 31, 101
Fownes, Peter 103
Frohman, Jesse 47

Gahr, David 129
Gall, Sally 197
Gallela, Ron 89
Geiger, Michael 220
Goldsmith, Lynn 129
Goldsworth, Andy 128
Gopp, Gary 208
Garcia Rodero, Cristina 208
Greenberg, Jill 131
Grison, Hervé 91
Gorson. H. Arthur 44
Guzman 229

Hales-Tooke, Hugh 226
Hall, Steve 139
Hamilton, James 115
Hanaver, Mark 20, 87
Hardin, Ted 24
Harpur, Jerry 222
Hawkins, Ken 208
Heffernan, Terry 94
Heinser, Thomas 139,
Heisler, Gregory 46, 74, 182,
  207
Henriksen, Poul Ib 105, 121
Higgins Jr. Chester 191

Index

Hitz, Evans 194
Hiro 44, 46, 187, 195
Holz, George 49, 95
Holmgen, Robert 180
Hood, Robin 84
Holbrooke, Andrew 207
Horst 27, 45, 90, 209
Hudson, Maxwell 210

Iacono, John 26
Iooss, Walter Jr. 186
Irish, Len 94, 185
Isaac, John 146, 188

Jones, John 32, 119, 192
Juau 137

Kazhdan, Naum 66
Katzenstein, David 44
Keler, Alain 101
Kelly, Paula 110
Kern, Geof 86, 119, 135, 183,
    184, 218
Kinmonth, Rob 215
Klein, Matthew 144
Klien, Diana 96
Kretschmer, Hugh 195

Lacombe, Brigitte 27, 46, 221
Lambot, Ian 140
Langer, Jason 145
Lee, Monica 144
Leibowitz, Annie 38, 44, 129
Levy, Karen 57
Lieberath, Frederick 92
Lindbergh, Peter 47, 48, 72, 92,
    126, 127, 224
Llewellyn, Michael 194
Lloyd, John 88
Lloyd, R. Ian 109
Lopez, Nola 172
Lowe, Paul 207
Ludes, Wolfgang 111
Ludwigsson, Hakan 124

Magnum 35, 114
Mahurin, Matt 96
Mankowitz, Gered 98
Mann, Sally 32, 192
Mapplethorpe, Robert 52
Mark, Mary Ellen 44, 136, 186,
    200, 206, 213,
Marsico, Dennis 100, 137, 196
Martin, Rick 208
Markus, Kurt 38
Matsumara, Glenn 113
Matrix 101
Matura, Ned 45,
McArthur, Pete 34, 94
McDonald, Michele 67

McDonough, John W. 99, 186
McGlynn, David 188, 189
McDermott & McGough 187
McKeown, Robert 95
Meier, Raymond 193, 216, 217,
    221
Mera, Masan 142, 143
Meuwenhuijs, V.E. 104
Michals, Duane 59, 71
Miller, Peter Reade 26
Misrach, Richard 125, 219
Montgomery, Wilbur 100
Moore, Suzi 146
Moore, Terrance 146
Moskowitz, Karen 30, 115
Mudford, Grant 27

Nachtwey, James 198
Neleman, Hans 205
Neuman, Arnold 105, 187
Newbury, Jeffery 86, 204

O'Brien, Michael 146, 189
O'Neill, Michael 33
Ockenfels 3, Frank W. 22, 87,
    98, 119, 210
Olson, Rosanne 55
Osborne, Bruce 132
Otte, Sylvia 32, 46, 149, 184,
    189
Outline 210

Parry, Nigel 190
Pearson, Victoria 49, 123
Penn, Irving 185
Perrin, Giles 53
Peterson, Grant 223
Pierce, Larry 100
Pokress, Dave 18
Porto, Jim 106
Preston, Neal 129

Quesada, Alex 26

Rand, Marvin 29
Raphan, Benita 132
Rattner, Robert 194
Ray, Bill 129
Reed Forsman, John 58
Regnier, Mike 102
Ressmeyer, Roger 85
Richards, Mark 208
Richardson, Alan 197
Richardson, Jim 146
Richardson, Martin 109
Ritts, Herb 38, 44, 83
Robert, Francois 43
Robledo, Maria 130
Rogers, Art 129
Rogers Neil 49

Rolston, Matthew 27, 45, 90,
    209,
Roversi, Paolo 88, 197

Saint-Loubert Bié, Jérome 55
Salgado, Sebastiao 199
Samuel, Deborah 61, 88
Saxberg, Nancy 88
Schiffman, Bonnie 44
Schnept, James 46
Schumann, Michael 208
Schutzer, Paul 129
Seliger, Mark 19, 21, 38, 98
Severson, John 82
Sherman, Steve 25
Simons, Chip 101
Smale, Brian 75, 184, 188
Solomon, Chuck 134
Staedler, Lance 138
Steinberg, Jim 100
Steele, Chris 207
Stevenson, Monica 140
Stoller, Ezra 20, 29
Strong, Tom 43
Suou, Anthony 214

The Bettmann Archive 141
Teller, Juergen 183
Testino, Mario 47, 48, 81, 92
Thurnher, Jeffrey 206
Trotter, John 207
Tucker, Mark 58, 63, 111, 112,
    189
Turin, Miranda 64
Turnley, David 146, 208

Underwood, Steve 62

Valeri, Mike 30
Van Antwerp, Jack 102
Van-S, Mark 115
Vereen, Dixie D. 34
Verde, Anthony 149
Verhufen, Hans 27
Veronsky, Frank 101
Verde, Anthony 149
Visages (Ritts) 44
von Unwerth, Ellen 183

Walker, Bradford 194
Warchol, Paul 47, 48
Watson, Albert 38, 78, 97, 99,
    100, 120, 138, 181, 182, 183,
    185, 228
Watson, Norman 71
Watson, Stuart 197
Weber, Bruce 38, 129
Wegman, William 95, 190
Well, Danielle 147, 191
Werthimer, Alfred 44

West, Bill 29
Westenberger, Theo 46
Wharton, David 75
Whitehead, Dauna 215
Willardt, Kenneth 194
Winters, Dan 85, 118, 132, 136,
    190, 212
Wippermann, Scott 69
Witkowski, Bob 208
Wojcik, James 71
Wolf, Bruce 131

Yamada, Toyohiro 31
Yoan 195

Photo Editors

Alberts, Heather 25
Albright, Alex 50

Baker, John 85
Baker Burrows, Barbara 50, 129,
    208
Barker, John 74, 86, 204, 205
Bartholomay, Lucy 67
Berthet, Jacqueline 68
Black, Bill 100, 137, 196
Braughtigan, Doris 20, 86, 87,
    125, 184

Calhoun, Catherine 84
Charlton, Aldona 69
Colihan, Jane 204

Doherty, Melanie 62
Douglas Brothers, The 53
Dunn, Mary 20, 46, 86, 87, 125,
    148, 149, 184, 206

Evans, Larry 196

Fahrenholz 133
Fishmann, Dianne 111
Frank, Karen 182, 184, 195, 207
Friend, David 207

Getsey, Kathy 186
Goknar, Esin 193, 216
Goldberger, Susan 185, 222
Goldburg, Margery 24
Goodman, Leslie 185
Gostin, Nicki 67, 134

Hess, Charles 200
Horan, Betsy 18, 87, 206

Jacobson, Mark 86
Jean-Louis, Galie 114

Kelly, Paula 56
Klech, Kathleen 219, 220, 221
Kluetmeier, Heinz 26, 186
Kono, Carol 58
Kratochvil, Laurie 19, 38, 44,
    83, 97, 98, 99, 120, 181, 182,
    185, 201, 209

McGovern, Tom 35
Meyer, Sabine 101
Mikich, Tripp 180
Mullarkey, Karen 99, 134, 186
Needleman, Deborah 34, 119,
    154

Pleasant, Anastasia 46
Pond, Greg 85, 183, 226, 228,
    229

Rank, Jerry J. 84
Ress, Laura 79, 111
Romanelli, Carmin 101
Romero, Michelle 149, 184
Rosenberg, Howard 66
Rowntree, Dirk 33
Ryan, Kathy 32, 33, 118, 119,
    147, 189, 190, 191, 192, 198,
    199

Saint-Loubert Bié, Jérome 55
Schaps, Jordan 24
Schlesinger, Kate 40
Shea, Mary 208
Sobel, Shana 186, 210
Stephenson, Michele 214
Stout, D.J. 135, 136, 212, 213

Publications

a/r/c Architectural Research
    and Criticism 22
Abitare 156
Adweek 101
American Enterprise, The 108
American Health 194
American Heritage 84, 204
American Photo 45
Anchorage Daily News 30, 114,
    115
Architectural Record 27, 51,
    139, 140
Art & Auction 187, 215
Aspen Aces & Eights 84

Atlantic Monthly, The 124, 156,
    169

Bloomberg Magazine 175
Boston Globe, The 69
Boston Globe Magazine, The 31,
    67, 117, 164
Boston Globe, The/Special
    Section 31, 68, 70, 117,
Brandweek 101
Bride's & Your New Home 220
Buzz 200

Calligraphy Review 28
CIO 102
Clio Brochure 102
Community Partnership of
    Santa Clara County Annual
    Report 63
Computer Reseller News 51
Computerworld 151
Condé Nast Traveler 27, 124,
    125, 148, 149, 151, 169, 219,
    220, 221
Corrections Corporation of
    America Annual Report 189
Country America 84
Creem 84

Dance Ink 40
Details 85, 157, 166, 183, 226,
    228, 229
Diabetes Forecast 102, 103
Digital News 54, 83, 110, 122,
    222, 145
Dimensions 1992 62
Discover 74, 85, 86, 170, 183,
    205
Discovery 109

Eastsideweek 30, 115
Ego 103
Elle Décor 45, 217, 221, 222
Entertainment Weekly 20, 81,
    86, 87, 125, 148, 149, 157,
    171, 184, 206
Esquire 18, 19, 22, 87, 157, 206,
    218
European Travel & Life 194

Forbes FYI 52, 103, 140, 141,
    161
Fortune 150
Four Seasons, Hotels and
    Resorts Magazine 88
Frankfurter Allgemeine
    Magazin 176

Garbage 75, 88
Glass 52

GQ 158, 182, 184, 195, 207
Graphis 28, 105, 121, 141, 142,
    143, 144, 187, 188

Harper's Bazaar 47, 48, 72, 80,
    81, 88, 89, 90, 92, 93, 126,
    127, 128, 197, 224, 227
Hat Life Directory 69
Health 94, 158, 172, 184
Hemispheres 48, 76, 94, 128
Here & Now 55
Hippocrates 105
House and Garden 185, 222
House Beautiful 195
How 24

Irregulomadaire 55

Kaplan Rules Cards 64
Kids Discover 150

LA Style 90, 91, 177
Los Angeles Times Magazine 21,
    31, 118, 215
LA Weekly 66
Lear's "Connection" Newsletter
    56, 110
Lida Baday Newsletter 57
Life 50, 94, 129, 207, 208
Life in Medicine 77
Lyric Opera Brochure 57

Macworld 161, 188, 195, 203
Magazine Week 78
Martha Stewart Living 49, 123,
    130, 131, 223
Men's Journal 49, 94, 95, 185
Metropolis 95, 131, 132
Minnesota Guide 30
Mohawk Paper Promotion 43,
    91
Mother Jones 22, 95

Natur 133
New York 24, 95
NewYork Times Arts & Leisure,
    The 35, 189
New York Times Styles, The 66
New York Times Magazine, The
    31, 32, 33, 71, 118, 119, 146,
    147, 164, 168, 177, 189, 190,
    191, 192, 197, 198, 199
New Yorker, The 211
Newsweek 22, 23, 148, 150, 211
North Carolina Literary Review
    50

Otis School of Art and Design 58
Outside 173, 196

P4 Magazine 53
Parenting 180
PC World 96
Person to Person 79, 111
Philadelphia Inquirer, The 35
Philadelphia Inquirer Magazine,
    The 164
Playboy 159
Popular Science 133
Print 28
Progressive Architecture 20, 29
Psychology Today 173,

Ray Gun 24, 82, 96, 159
Rolling Stone 19, 38, 41, 44, 83,
    97, 98, 99, 120, 159, 160, 181,
    182, 185, 201, 209

Saint Francis Hospital Spirit 29
Salon Styling with Vidal
    Sassoon 111
San Francisco Focus 160, 210
San Francisco International
    Airport 65
Scholastic Scope 106
Self 185
Shiny 33
Show Offs 58, 111, 112
Signatures of the Body 59
Snake Eyes 24
Special Report 161, 174, 185
Spin 186, 210
Sports Illustrated 26, 99, 134,
    155, 161, 186
SPY 67, 99, 134, 151
Stanford Magazine 111, 113,
    145, 162
Stanford Medicine 113, 162
Steamboat 100
Subjective Reasoning 1 60
Subjective Reasoning 2 60
Subjective Reasoning 3 59

TDC 29
Texas Monthly 135, 136, 212,
    213
Time 137, 214
Time International 18, 26, 27
Time Warner Inc. 1992 Annual
    Report 64
Total TV 24
Traces 100
Travel Holiday 100, 137, 174,
    196

U&lc 53, 105, 106, 144
Us 138, 187

Value Newsletter 188
Varbusiness 107

VH1 Capabilities Brochure 65
Village Voice, The 35, 115, 162, 163
Vibe 100, 138
Vogue 193, 216

W 27, 202
Wall Street Journal Reports, The 163
Washington Lawyer, The 108
Washington Post Magazine, The 34, 119, 154, 165, 197
Washington Times, The 116
Wordperfect for Windows 107, 108, 162
Wordperfect Magazine 175
World 146, 188
World Tour 42, 61, 113, 114

Young Sisters and Brothers 25

Zapata Brochure 61
Zoo Views 62

CMP Publications 51, 107
Condé Nast Publishing Co., Inc. 27, 85, 124, 125, 148, 149, 151, 157, 158, 166, 169, 182, 183, 184, 185, 193, 194, 207, 216, 219, 220, 221, 222, 226, 228, 229
Creem 84

Dance Ink, Inc. 40
Discovery Publishing, Inc. 29
Disney Magazine Publishing 72, 85, 86, 170, 183, 204, 205
Dovetale Publishers 75, 88
Dow Jones & Company, Inc. 163

East Carolina University, Greenville, NC 50
Emphasis Co. Ltd, Hong Kong 109
Entertainment Weekly, Inc. 20, 46, 81, 86, 87, 125, 148, 149, 171, 184, 206

F&W Publications 24
Fairchild Publications 27, 202
Fantagraphic Books 24
Fishman Creative Associates 111
Forbes, Inc. 52, 103, 104, 140, 141, 161
Foundation for National Progress 22, 95
Frankfurter Allgemeine Magazin 176

Graphis US, Inc. 28, 104, 105, 121, 141, 142, 143, 144, 187, 188

Hachette Magazines, Inc. 45, 217, 221, 222
Health 94, 158, 172, 184
Hearst Corporation, The 18, 19, 47, 48, 72, 80, 81, 87, 88, 89, 90, 92, 93, 126, 127, 128, 157, 195, 197, 206, 218, 224, 227,
Hippocrates 105

Indiana Historical Society 100
International Typeface Corporation 53, 105, 106
Irregulomadaire 55

K-III Magazines 24, 95, 194
Kids Discover 150
KPMG Peat Marwick Communications 146, 188
KQED, Inc. 160, 210

LA Weekly 66
Lear's Publishing 56, 110
Los Angeles Times 21, 31, 118, 215

Macworld Communications 161, 188, 195, 203
Magazine Group, The 108
Magazine Week, Inc. 78
Mariah Publications Corporation 173, 196
McGraw-Hill Publicatons 27, 51, 139, 140
Mead Paper 59
Meredith Corporation 84
Michael Bloomberg 176

New York Times, The 31, 32, 33, 35, 66, 71, 118, 119, 146, 147, 164, 168, 177, 189, 190, 191, 192, 197, 198, 199
Newsweek, Inc. 22, 23, 148, 150, 211

Pace Communication 76, 94, 128
Paige Publications, Inc. 25, 48
PCW Communications, Inc. 96
Penton Publishing 20, 29
Philadelphia Inquirer, The 35, 164
Physician Services of America 77
Playboy 159
Polaroid UK 53

Ray Gun 25, 82, 96, 159
RC Publications 28
Readers Digest Publications 100, 137, 174, 194, 196
Ringier Verlag GMbh 133

Sasquatch Publishing 30, 115
Scholastic, Inc. 106
Shiny International 33
Simpson Paper Company 62
Spy Corporation 67, 99, 134, 151
Stanford Alumni Association 111, 113, 145, 162
Star Tribune 30
Straight Arrow Publishers, Inc. 19, 38, 44, 49, 83, 94, 95, 97, 98, 99, 120, 138, 159, 160, 181, 182, 185, 187, 201, 209
Sussex Publishers 173

Texas Monthly 135, 136, 212, 213
Time Inc. 26, 27

Time Inc. Magazine Company 26, 94, 99, 129, 134, 155, 161, 186, 214
Time Inc. Magazine Group 150
Time Inc. Ventures 123
Time Publishing Ventures 49, 130, 131, 223
Time /Warner, Inc. 18, 50, 129, 137, 207, 208
Times Mirror 133
Total TV, Inc. 25

Village Voice Publishing Corporation 35, 115, 162, 163

Washington Post Co., The 34, 119, 154, 165, 197
Washington Times, The 116
Whittle Communications 161, 174, 186
WordPerfect Publishing 107, 108, 162, 175

Suarez, Edna 115
Sullivan, Kate 194
Swan, Bill 90, 91

Tanaka, Karen 34, 197
Thackaberry, Lisa 21, 31, 118, 215
Torresyap, Fay 150

Vogliano, Ernest 84

Waters, Celia 208
Whitfield, Cathy 109
Wieseltier Fattal, Thea 138

Publishers

Abitare 156
Advance Publication 211
Adweek, L.P. 101
American Diabetes Association 102
American Express Publishing 90, 91, 177
American Heritage 84, 204
Anchorage Daily News 30, 114, 115
Art & Auction Joint Ventures 187, 215
Aspen Aces and Eights, Inc. 84
Atlanta Art and Design, Toronto 88
Atlantic Monthly, The 124, 156, 169
Atlas of the City 22

Bellerophon Publications, Inc. 95, 131, 132
Boston Globe Publishing Co., The 31, 67, 68, 69, 70, 117, 164
Buzz, Inc. 200

C.W. Publishing, Inc. 151
Camouflage Associates 186, 210,
Champion International 59, 60
CIO Publishing 102,

Design Firm Studio

Atlanta Art and Design, Toronto
54, 83, 110, 122, 145

Carson Design, David 25, 82,
96, 159
Concrete Design
Communications, Inc. 57, 61
Context Inc. 29
Cook Design, Ken 188

Design Writing Research 40
Dickens Design, Holly 119
Doherty Design, Melanie 62
Doubling Communication 111
Drentell Doyle Partners 60

Ellis Design 58, 63, 111, 112,
189

Fabella, Ted 103
Frankfurt Gips Balkind 64

Gee Design, Earl 63
Guarnaccia, Steven 156

Hopkins/Baumann 150
Hornall Anderson Design
Works, Inc. 55

Isley Design, Alexander 52,
103, 104, 140, 141, 161
Isely and Clark Design 108

Johnson Design, Dean 100

Koepke Design Group 42, 61,
100, 113, 114, 138

Menchin, Scott 30
Morla Design 65
Morris Design Associates, David
69
Muller + Company 102

Parham-Santana, Inc. 64, 65
Pentagam Design, London 53
Pentagram Design, NYC 43, 48,
52, 53, 59, 60, 76, 91, 94, 104,
128
Pentagram Design, S.F., CA 48,
76, 94, 128
Petrick Design 79, 111
Ph.D 58
Poulin Design, Richard 62

Pushpin Group, Inc., The 28,
105, 106, 176

Rank, Jerry J. 84
Rosen, Jonathon 157

Steamboat Communications
Group 100
Studio W 25
Suzuki, Inc., Tom 102, 103

Travel Holiday 100, 196

WBMG, Inc. 53, 78, 106, 144

Clients

Athens Paper 58, 111, 112
American Diabetes Association
102, 103

Calder, Kent 100
Cathay Pacific Airways 109
Champion International 59, 60
Crysler, Greg 22
Comprehensive Health
Education Foundation 55
Community Partnership of
Santa Clara County 63
Corrections Corporation 63, 189
Creative Club of Atlanta 103

Digital Equiptment of Canada
83, 110, 122, 145

East Carolina University,
English Department 50

Foote, Cone, & Belding 79
Four Seasons Hotels and
Resorts 88

Hopper Paper 188

Irregulomadaire 55

Kaplan, Stanley H. Education
Center Ltd. 64

Mead Paper 59
Mohawk Paper Mills 43, 91

New York Experimental Glass
Workshop 52, 104

Otis School of Art and Design 58

Polaroid 53

Proctor and Gamble 111

San Francisco International
Airport 65
San Francisco Zoolological
Society 62
Simpson Paper Company 62

Time Warner Inc. 64

United Airlines 48, 76, 94, 128

VH1 Channnel (MTV Networks)
65